TWELVE DYNAMIC SHIFTS
for Transforming
YOUR CHURCH

TWELVE DYNAMIC SHIFTS
for Transforming
YOUR CHURCH

E. Stanley Ott

William B. Eerdmans Publishing Company
Grand Rapids, Michigan / Cambridge, U.K.

© 2002 Wm. B. Eerdmans Publishing Co.
All rights reserved

Wm. B. Eerdmans Publishing Co.
255 Jefferson Ave. S.E., Grand Rapids, Michigan 49503 /
P.O. Box 163, Cambridge CB3 9PU U.K.
www.eerdmans.com

Printed in the United States of America

07 06 05 04 03 02   7 6 5 4 3 2 1

Library of Congress Cataloging-in-Publication Data

Ott, E. Stanley, 1948-
Twelve dynamic shifts for transforming your church /
E. Stanley Ott.
p.   cm.
Includes bibliographical references.
ISBN 0-8028-4949-0 (pbk.: alk. paper)
1. Church renewal. I. Title.

BV600.3.O77 2002
250 — dc 21

2002024470

Dedicated to Harry A. Fifield, D.D.,
whose question
"Are you thronging Jesus or touching him?"
continues to stir my heart.
(Mark 5:31)

CONTENTS

PREFACE

What is your church like today? Perhaps your congregation is experiencing wonderful energy and growth. Or perhaps it was established some time ago and is now experiencing a loss of activity and vitality. Whatever your church is like now, consider the possibility that God has an exciting future for your church! Seek fresh vision from God. Trust God for wisdom, guidance, and courage. And act to transform your congregation's life by God's grace.

What steps might you take to bring about this transformation? In this book I will discuss twelve dynamic shifts in thinking and practice that you can use in the process of bringing new vision and fresh energy into the life of your church. Although a transformational vision leads to a vast array of potential shifts in the life of congregational ministry, the shifts I outline here touch on a variety of matters essential to congregational life. Each one can lead to new energy in the life of your church!

One of the greatest challenges we face in the transformation of our congregations is the tension we may feel between familiar ways of doing things and new approaches that increasingly seem to be key to attracting new congregants. While we want to show honor to the people and the programs that have served our congregation well in the past, we also want to look for the shifts in vision and practice that will keep us moving out of old routines and into new life. Sometimes these shifts will feel a little unfamiliar or a bit risky. But the alternative is simply to run in place, to keep busy maintaining the status quo, but go nowhere. William Barclay tells of a time that Rudyard Kipling saw General Booth of the Salvation Army come aboard a ship to the pounding of tambourines. Kipling, who had more traditional tastes, profoundly disliked the noisy music and said so. "Young man," Booth replied, "if I thought I could win one more soul for Christ by standing on my head and beating a tambourine with my feet, I would learn how to do it." Now that may seem a bit extreme, but I must say I like Booth's attitude, that openness to the practices that will most effectively win new hearts for Christ.

Jim Tozer is the founding pastor and former senior pastor of Covenant Presbyterian Church in West Lafayette, Indiana. He is my mentor and a friend of the heart which whom I had the privilege of serving for many years. He and I attended many seminars and congregational training events over the years. Each time we'd come home with a notebook full of ideas and minds brimming with plans. Jim used to say that if we would apply just one major idea or insight from each such event, our ministry would be profoundly affected. And he was right. In our day of information overload, it is all too easy to look at numerous potential changes in church life and affirm the validity of all of them yet actually undertake none of them. That's why, as I outline the twelve dynamic shifts, I recommend that you choose one or two shifts that appear to be of greatest significance to your ministry at the present time and work to make them a reality. Then move on to the next shift that's most important to your congregation's needs.

Preface

I have written this book especially for pastors and all who share in the leadership of their congregation. I urge you to read this book with a mind open to fresh guidance from the Spirit of God. Perhaps you will receive an entirely new vision. Perhaps you will be led to modify or reshape the ministry that you and your congregation are presently engaged in. I love the promise that James offered when he wrote, "If any of you lacks wisdom, he should ask God, who gives generously to all without finding fault, and it will be given to him" (1:5). Pray for wisdom and vision. Study this material with others who have vision, with those who will join you in thinking and praying about these matters. And take action. As 1 Chronicles 28:20 exhorts us, "Be strong and courageous, and do the work."

*   *

Many people have helped me with this book along the way. I am thankful for the encouragement of my wife, Ann Marie, and for the warm fellowship of the Pleasant Hills Church — together we have shared in the transitions I describe in the following pages. I am also thankful for the fellowship of the Pittsburgh Presbytery, to whom this material was first presented. I am grateful to Ben C. Johnson for his warm encouragement, and to Sam Eerdmans for his support in the publication of this material. I am also grateful for the pleasure of working with my editor, Mary Hietbrink, and for the good help of my assistant, Diane Davis. For them all I have great affection and gratitude.

CHAPTER ONE

The Church in Transition

In American culture today, huge shifts in expectations, life-style, and the understanding of truth are radically changing how people perceive the church and their very receptivity to the gospel. The advent of terrorist acts on American soil and rising levels of anxiety and uncertainty appear to have inspired fresh interest in finding hope, coping with fear, and finding something to believe in. Perhaps we are on the leading edge of a new "Awakening."

But even before these unsettling events, major changes in our culture were well underway. Christendom, the era in which the church stood at the center of the culture, is history. We are in a post-Christendom, post-modern world. In fact, a recent edition of *REV* magazine, an outstanding periodical on congregational and spiritual vitality, featured an article on post–post-modernism — and many of us are still trying to grasp what "post-modern" means.[1] Indeed, things are changing so rapidly in American culture today that it's

---

1. Sally Morgenthaler, "Is Post-Modernism Passe?" *REV* 5, no. 1 (September/October 2001), pp. 68-75. For an excellent treatment of ways a congregation may adjust its ministry to a post-modern culture, see Leonard Sweet, *Post-Modern Pilgrims* (Nashville: Broadman & Holman, 2000).

difficult for most of us to keep up. In this fast-paced, increasingly impersonal world, people hunger for personal experience, personal relationships, and personal involvement.

How should the church respond? The church is like a ship on a stormy sea without reference points from land or sky with which to steer a course. We have to use the "internal guidance" system that the Spirit of God offers to every body of believers, vital signs of a biblically consistent vision for ministry that we may implement in whatever culture we find ourselves. Significantly, these days are not unlike the days of the early church, when the church was not the center of our culture, and when there were many competing voices clamoring for people's spiritual allegiance. But because of our culture's great hunger for meaning, the church has an unparalleled opportunity to introduce people to Jesus Christ and involve them in the fellowship and support of the Body of Christ.

Michael Warden, writing for Leadership Network,[2] describes the church's situation and opportunity clearly:

> In the last half of the twentieth century, the American religious landscape was transformed. Commitment to traditional church structures steadily waned, while at the same time our hunger for spiritual fulfillment inched its way into the forefront of the cultural dialog. For the first time in our history as a nation, the concept of Truth began to lose its status as an independent reality. Instead,

2. Leadership Network is a private foundation. They define their ministry this way: "Our mission is to accelerate the emergence of effective churches. Effective churches develop leadership teams; equip and deploy the people of God for service; understand and engage the culture; build authentic community; and achieve missional impact" (www.leadnet.org).

Truth became relative, dependent on an individual's circumstance or perspective.

This is a sign of the times . . . only one among many. The culture is shifting. And many of the established paradigms by which churches have operated for decades can no longer support a populace that is looking for Truth outside the "box" created by our predecessors. By necessity, the twenty-first-century church is becoming more flexible and organic, adapting and changing to engage the culture that surrounds it.

This new environment is giving rise to a fundamental "re-design" of how the church carries out its mission. To be effective, churches once thought (and many still think) that all they needed to do was maintain certain expected church programs, provide a sanctuary where members could gather for worship, perhaps send out work teams into the community, or support missionaries at various locations around the globe. Effective missional churches in today's culture are breaking new ground, trying new approaches, and going back to the blueprint provided in Scripture to show them how to become an authentic "city on a hill that cannot be hidden."[3]

The "saltiness" of the Gospel has not changed, but society is changing rapidly. As Warden makes clear, the church must change too if its message is to be heard and is to help. And now is the time: our evangelistic and disciple-making opportunities have never been greater. The church has a great message in the Gospel of Jesus Christ, and now it is needed more than ever — to speak to the brokenness of soci-

3. Warden, "The Missional Church: Being the Church in Today's World," *NEXT* 6, 2d quarter (2000), p. 1.

ety and to respond to the deep spiritual hunger we see everywhere. People still love, still hurt, still hope, and they still need to be shown love and respect.

What does it mean to be the church today? A central conviction of the Reformation was expressed by the Scots Confession of 1560, which declared three signs of the true church in which Christ is present: "the true preaching of the word of God," "the right administration of the sacraments of Christ Jesus," and "ecclesiastical discipline uprightly ministered."[4] We still affirm this conviction. At the same time, we all know of devoted, hard-working congregations that still lose members, struggle to sustain their organization, and worry about their future. Wherever you find yourself as a church, know this for sure: God has an exciting, life-building vision for the whole church and for your congregation. Ask for the faith to believe it, the grace to see it, and the courage to act on it.

Intense and demanding issues face many mainline congregations who are seriously interested in being part of a vital and vigorous fellowship of God's people. While it is true that some congregations in rapidly growing areas seem to have more people than they know what to do with, the vast majority of mainline congregations find themselves on a numerical plateau, trying to relate to the diversity of tastes and opinions both within the church and in the surrounding community.

Tom Brokaw's best-seller, *The Greatest Generation,* profiles the generation that was born in the 1920s; coincidentally, 1920 was the year my own father was born. You don't have to read much of Brokaw's book to realize how great the attitude shift has been between the generations in virtually every facet of daily life. In times gone by, the generational

4. The Scots Confession, chapters 18 and 25.

equivalents of the World War II builders, the Baby Boomers, and the Generation X'ers all worshiped together in the normal mix of any congregation. To varying degrees, mainline congregations could count on everyone being there and having their needs met. This is no longer true. At the same time, such congregations must cope with the changing environment of the culture. Further, not infrequently they find themselves in competition (if I may use that word) with vigorous congregations that tend to attract the most progressive and capable leaders from the surrounding region.

Congregations that grow genuine disciples, that effectively meet human needs, that help people grow in faith, that create a place to belong with friendships of the heart and ways to serve — they must work successfully across the generations as well as retain the participation of present members. Those of us who pastor and all of us who lead these congregations face two challenges: (1) showing love and honor to those who have been among us for generations — indeed, whose lifelong investment in our congregations has sustained them, and (2) adjusting our ministry to draw the lesser churched and the unchurched to Jesus Christ and into the fellowship of God's people.

For some of us, the dynamics of change required will be an "easy sell," with great affirmation of new vision. Others of us will face exceedingly complex dynamics in the effort to move our congregations in the direction of new life. Most of us are familiar with the amazing growth and imaginative ministry of the Willow Creek Community Church, located in South Barrington, Illinois. Each week it reaches about 20,000 people through worship and other ministries. The congregation was begun by Bill Hybels and has been recognized for its innovations aimed at reaching those with no church background.

Imagine that at some time in the future you are Pastor Hybels' successor at Willow Creek, with its thousands of worshipers. Suppose that you are given the mandate (for whatever surprising reason) to change the Sunday morning "Seeker Service" that defines the Willow Creek culture into a Mozart- and Bach-based service — without losing anyone.

Impossible, you say? Well, it would certainly be challenging! Many of us face that challenge in reverse in mainline churches today: how to expand the scope of our ministries to attract people of different tastes while keeping those members we have — without burning out or being taken out in the process. That doesn't necessarily mean that we will introduce "seeker services" into our congregations, but it does mean that reaching people today will require many of us to make major adjustments in our ministries.

Transition is not a strange concept for the church. Every congregation finds itself in the midst of some sort of transition. It may be as simple as the transition of people rotating on and off various boards and committees. It could be the transition that occurs when a once-vital congregation is losing momentum and members. But I want to offer a new definition of the transitional congregation — a church in transition to a positive, future-embracing vision that says, "We have not yet experienced this congregation's greatest ministry. Let us bless what God has done among us and add the ministry we believe will touch another circle of people."

People within churches that have reached a plateau know that things don't have to remain the same. Evidence of successful change is everywhere. There are many vital congregations scattered around virtually every metropolitan area which, though they reflect a diversity of theological viewpoints and cultural styles, nevertheless share many common characteristics. Vital churches of all sizes everywhere evidence vigorous worship, winsome discipleship, fellowship in large and small groups, and ministry as both program and personal lifestyle. They understand themselves as sent, in all humility, by God to pursue the work of Jesus Christ in the world.

Some may ask, Why can't we just maintain things the way they are? It is true that some things should be sustained. Most congregations have some activities — for example, a women's Bible study or a ministry of compassion — that have been bringing honor to Christ and building up people for many years. Yet many of the standard programs of the church are out of touch with people today. Pastors and congregational members alike are looking everywhere for "clues" about how to renew their churches effectively. Look at the vast numbers of people within denominational settings (and across the theological spectrum) who are going to congregations, seminars, and vendors outside of their denominational families and seminaries for training and resources in support of pastoral care, Bible study, small groups, music and worship shifts, short-term missions, Christian education, and overall vision for a vital church.

Furthermore, many changes in our culture call us to rethink what we are doing and how effective we really are. Here are three critical changes particularly important to the church:

- The culture has definitely shifted away from a church-centered society.
- We are in the most musically diverse age in the history of humanity.
- The demands required to cope with life appear to be on the increase.

In *Prepare Your Church for the Future,* Carl George reviews the ministry of the traditional church, which emphasizes the pastor as primary caregiver, and the programs of many large sub-congregation groups. He contends, "The congregation paradigm describes most of North American religions and it's failing. Why? Because it's not prepared to cope with the quality of turmoil people are experiencing in their personal lives."[5] Sitting in rows listening to a speaker in audience-oriented programming used to be standard in the church and adequate to our lives. It is no longer adequate, by itself, to meet needs and grow disciples.

In his book *The Spirit of the Disciplines,* Dallas Willard offers these thought-provoking comments:

> Think of how we exclaim over and mark as rarities those who seem truly to have the power and spirit of Christ about them. The very way the bright exceptions stand out proves the rule that the guidance given by the church is not even counted on by the church itself to produce the kinds of people we know it should produce.
>
> No one is surprised, though we sometimes complain, when faithful church members do not grow to maturity in Christ. With steady regularity we fail to realize the "abundance of life" the gospel clearly promises. We know this to be painfully true. Experience has taught us this, though we may bravely try to ignore it.
>
> This failure has nothing to do with the usual divisions between Christians, such as that between Protestant and Catholic or between liberal and conservative

---

5. George, *Prepare Your Church for the Future* (Grand Rapids: Revell, 1991), p. 69.

or between charismatic and non-charismatic, for the failure is shared on all sides.[6]

Willard's observations are on point, I think: the church is not adequately addressing the turmoil in people's lives or helping them develop their spiritual maturity, and it needs to rectify these weaknesses. With all of its worship services, its Christian education programs, and its fellowship and service programs, the mainline church has somehow been ineffective in developing the kind of discipleship indispensable for both a vital faith and the vital church. We have assumed the discipleship of our congregants rather than working to lovingly, deliberately develop faith, hope, and love in their lives.

This book is about blessing and adding. It is about the clear and confident giving of honor to the people, programs, and events that have been God's instruments, up until now, for bringing spiritual vitality to the people and into the church. It is also about assertively advancing ministry by adding those emphases and initiatives that will give peace and hope to people when they experience personal turmoil and introduce them to the spiritual disciplines of genuine and growing discipleship.

This book aims to help you as pastors and other leaders conceive a clear vision to help your congregations move in the direction of transformational ministry. The groundwork for a vision requires you to think through the following:

1. the issues raised in this book
2. the present state of your congregation's life

6. Willard, *The Spirit of the Disciplines: Understanding How God Changes Lives* (San Francisco: Harper & Row, 1988), pp. 31-32.

3. where you would like to see your congregation go and
   grow with God's help

   In the next chapter I look at some of the characteristics
of the transformational congregation. In the subsequent
chapters I discuss twelve specific shifts your congregation
can make to "go and grow with God's help."
   The Spirit gives us our particular ministry. Pray, asking
God for wisdom, insight, and courage. Read the following
material, thoughtfully reflect on it, then jot down a few
ideas and "next steps" on paper. When you complete this assignment, join with others who are also eager to see your
congregation develop a new vitality and begin the process of
discerning and planning what you will actually do.

CHAPTER TWO

Your Congregation Today

Oh, to be in a vigorous church! All of us want our congregations to be truly vital, full of life and vigor. Growing a vital church demands hard work, and it can be difficult to commit ourselves to that. But we know the alternative: a church with no vision and no vigor, a church with little that genuinely challenges our interior lives and motivates our practice of Christian spirituality in the home, community, and workplace.

None of us wants a dull, boring, lifeless, routine church if by God's grace we can change it. We long to have vigorous, need-responsive churches that are making a genuine and humble attempt to touch as many people as possible and to enable them to grow as winsome disciples of Jesus Christ. We want our churches to grow through this responsiveness. Although growth cannot always be measured in numbers, numbers are often meaningful, as Acts 16:5 indicates: "So the churches were strengthened in the faith and grew daily in numbers." We also have an interest in compassion, in bringing God's restoring love into our communities and the world. We want to help as many people as possible to glorify God and enjoy God forever.

Years ago when my brother, Jim, the youngest member

11

of our family, was a graduating senior in high school, my mother decided she could finally replace her old dining room table with a beautiful new one. The old table was pretty worn, bearing the scratches and watermarks from the four children who had grown up around it. If you looked at the surface carefully, you could see some math homework inscribed into the surface by one of us kids who forgot to put a placemat under the paper. That table had been at the center of much of our family's life.

Finally, on the appointed day, the doorbell rang. The men delivering the new table came in to remove the old table first. When my brother heard the noises coming from the dining room, he came flying up the stairs from the family room, raced through the living room into the dining room, and threw himself bodily on top of the old table, arms outstretched, fingers curling under one end of the table, and toes curling under the other end. "Noooo! Don't take it," he cried. "It's our family! This is where we were together. This is where we laughed and cried. Don't do it!" I would have felt exactly the same way if I had been there. That table had defined our family circle. But my mother, standing quietly to the side, was quite unmoved by this display. "Dear," she said, "the old furniture doesn't meet our needs anymore. We do have wonderful memories, but it's time to move on."

Mom reminded me of that incident the other day. Having just sold her home and moved into a condominium, she no longer needed that large table. Guess which child received the table? My brother, of course.

How clearly this incident depicts many of our churches today and the changes they face. It's time to move on, but acknowledging that and then doing it can be very difficult. In a way my brother spoke for the established church and its present practices when he cried, "Don't take it. It's our family!" Many of us have gathered around our congregation's "family table" for much of our lives, and many of our precious memories were made there. But is it time to broaden the family and its traditions? Maybe your congregation doesn't function as effectively as it could. Perhaps many of us, in fact, deny the diminishing state of our congregations because we love and value the traditions that have established them. But my mother's words to my brother remain relevant to the future vitality of our churches. She acknowledged the many happy memories associated with the old table but also declared, "It's time to move on."

A crisis in the mainline church really exists, a crisis much more extensive than is suggested by many of the issues that so frequently dominate the denominational agendas and religious debates of today. The crisis includes both personal spirituality (Trinitarian, biblically grounded spirituality) and congregational vitality. It is time to move on, to be grateful for the wonderful heritage of spiritual vitality that we have received and to begin doing the "new things" that by God's grace will bring about spiritual vitality in the future.

Three Types of Congregations

In this time of dynamic change in American culture and in American congregations, we see three basic types of congregational ministry: (1) traditional, (2) transitional, and (3) transformational. All three types of congregations and their particular forms of ministry may be vital if they are building disciples and meeting people's needs. While there are vital traditional congregations with exceptional leadership that do continue to thrive today, transitional and transformational congregations have discovered that the lifestyles and needs of people in their communities have shifted. They recognize that if the church is to regain members and grow in vitality, the practice of ministry that builds disciples and meet needs must shift as well.

In the remainder of this chapter I will first describe several key characteristics of both the traditional and the transformational congregations in order to compare and contrast their ministries with respect to the role of the pastor, the nature of the worship service, the usual participation of the members, the typical ministry involvement of the members, and the governance of the congregation. With this contrast in form clearly in mind, I will then explore the transitional congregation, which shares characteristics of both the traditional and the transformational ministry.

Traditional and Transformational Congregations: Key Differences

A *traditional* congregational ministry focuses on the pastor as the primary doer of ministry and thus the central teacher/preacher, leader, and caregiver. The pastor in a traditional church is often expected to be present at virtually every gathering of congregational groups. Frequently he or she is expected to visit members in their homes. In the transformational church, the pastor remains the primary preacher/teacher and leader but also shares leadership and plays a different role in care-giving. While such a pastor may continue to attend to some critical kinds of care, the majority of pastoral care shifts to the people themselves, who understand their role of caring for one another in small-group and face-to-face settings. Transformational congregations do not expect their pastors to show up at every group gath-

Characteristics of the Three Types of Churches

	Traditional	Transitional	Transformational
Pastor	The pastor is the primary doer of ministry — central preacher, leader, caregiver. He is expected to be present at most meetings.	← both →	The pastor is the primary leader and one of the central preachers. The pastor remains a caregiver in certain situations, but most care has shifted to the people.
Worship	Traditional worship services feature classical and traditional church music, church choirs, and traditional vestments as well as the particular liturgical elements of the individual church's tradition.	← both →	Transformational congregations may employ any of a variety of worship styles, such as the traditional service, the contemporary service, and the blended service.
Fellowship and Mission	Communal in emphasis. The members of the congregation experience fellowship by participating in committees and interest groups. Missions is one of the various programs of the church.	← both →	Communal and missional in emphasis. The congregation and each of its ministries reach those who are uninvolved and uncommitted, grow the relationship and nurture the spiritual growth of those participating, and send every person to ministry.

The people's participation	The people attend Sunday worship and participate in programs, typically on a low-commitment basis (Lyle Schaller).	← both →	The people attend Sunday worship and participate in small groups on a high-commitment basis. They are involved in programs on an "as interested" basis.
The people's ministry	The people serve on ruling board (session, vestry, council, board of deacons) and committees. Some teach, usher, handle a variety of tasks. Most members have no formal ministry at any given time.	← both →	The people embrace ministry as lifestyle: the use of spiritual gifts and a servant heart inside and outside the church. This means service within the congregation plus the understanding that all have been "sent" in all humility to do ministry in every place and at all times.
Governance	The ruling board members set policy and lead programs. The emphasis is on control.	← both →	The ruling board members identify the "defining" vision and practices of the congregation. The emphasis is on "permission-giving" — endorsing proposals consistent with the church's vision and practices.
	The majority of congregational activities are led by committees and solo leaders.		Ministry teams are the primary means of leadership for all ministries.

ering or to visit every home. They understand that the pastor's role is to develop the disciples and leaders who in turn lead the congregational groups and undertake much home visitation of those needing comfort and encouragement. The pastor is no longer the primary "do-er" of ministry but one who both shares ministry and devotes significant time to the training of congregants for their ministry at church, home, and the workplace.

Traditional worship services feature classical and traditional church music, church choirs, and traditional vestments as well as the particular liturgical elements of the individual church's tradition (such as creeds and the practice of the sacraments). In transformational congregations, any of a variety of worship styles may be found, from the traditional worship service just described, to the contemporary service featuring praise music and extended time for teaching and preaching, to the blended worship service that includes elements of both kinds of services. Regardless of style, worship services in the transformational congregation remain firmly rooted in their theological and liturgical tradition. A given congregation must base its worship style on what will best help all who gather there to worship Almighty God.

In traditional churches, typical involvement of the members in the life of the church includes attending worship and participating in programs, often on what Lyle Schaller, a leading authority on congregational vitality, calls a "low-commitment" basis. Such programs may include a women's association with circles and luncheons, a men's breakfast, a youth group, and deacons who engage in works of service and various support ministries, from Christian education to stewardship. The majority of traditional church programs are audience-oriented, with a group listening to a speaker.

Little in traditional programming provides opportunity for the average involved member to participate in face-to-face Bible study, sharing of one's personal life and experiences, or praying for one another. Transformational congregations, on the other hand, center their members' involvement in worship and in small groups on a high-commitment basis. Small groups provide personal friendships, loving care, opportunity for ministry to one another, and warm inspiration to grow in discipleship. In transformational churches, members gather in large groups for worship, teaching, and inspiration, *and* in small face-to-face groups where they are most fully known and deeply loved.

The ministry of members in a traditional congregation typically involves participation on a church board or a committee (with some functioning as Sunday school teachers, youth advisors, and ushers). If a member doesn't have a program assignment at a given time, this means that, with the exception of financial support of the church, he or she doesn't have a formal ministry in the church at that particular moment. The church that functions this way pays little more than lip service to the biblical concept that every member should be involved in ministry. On the other hand, the ministry of the people in transformational congregations involves the deliberate discovery of each person's passion and spiritual gifts for ministry and the intentional deployment of each person to that ministry of interest. It equips each person to carry out daily personal ministry to the individuals in his or her life. Ministry thus becomes a way of life, not merely a program that is run. As a result, ministry is no longer limited to a committee assignment and financial support. Transformational congregations develop a sense of "sent-ness" as the disciples of Christ: they come to understand themselves as sent, in all humility, to do ministry in every place and at all times. Every-member ministry becomes the norm, not just a nice-sounding motto. It becomes basic to the work of Christ in the congregation and through the congregation into the community and the world.

In a traditional congregation, the governing board — the elders and their equivalents — typically sets policy and administrates programs. In essence the elders function in a manner similar to that of staff members of a larger congregation. Each elder is involved in the leadership of a particular program or a committee assignment, such as Christian education, stewardship, or worship. As congregations grow numerically, we often see their governing board members continue to both set policy and run programs. Conversely, in larger transitional and transformational churches, the elders (or their equivalents) determine congregational purpose and operating policies, but they do not actually administrate programs. In these congregations, program and ministry are implemented by congregational members with a heart for ministry — with support, training, and encouragement from the pastoral staff and others in the congregation who lead.

In traditional congregations, the governing board tends to act as a "committee of the whole," attempting to solve every problem. In transformational congregations of all sizes, we see the governing board operating on a "permission-giving" basis. The board simply endorses proposals that are consistent with the defining vision and practices of the congregation. They trust the people proposing a particular kind of ministry to have done their homework and expect only to be kept informed of the progress of that ministry.

Traditional congregations are often somewhat self-absorbed, with the majority of activities geared for those who are already churched. Local and international missions are the responsibility of a "missions committee" and perhaps a few other programs within the life of the church. Transformational congregations, on the other hand, are inherently missional in nature, seeking to reach in significant and effective ways the people in their community with the good news and compassion of Jesus Christ. They make missional thinking a part of the vision of every ministry and activity within the congregation, not just the "missions committee."

Traditional ministry is typically led by committees or solo leaders. Committees place a premium on task accomplishment, with little emphasis on nurturing their discipleship or developing "koinonia" community among themselves. Solo leaders carry out their responsibilities until their passion wanes for the activity they lead or until they move on to other responsibilities, leaving those behind to scramble for new leadership. On the other hand, transformational ministry is led by ministry teams which are both communal and missional in nature. They give deliberate time and attention to their life together as a group of disciples as well as to the fulfillment of their common vision. They provide a continuity of leadership that is independent of the comings and goings of any one leader and a breadth of leadership that is greater than can be offered by the solo leader.

The Transitional Congregation

The *transitional* congregation seeks increased vitality as it shifts from traditional to transformational approaches. The members of a transitional congregation hold a wide range of opinions about what the pastor and the church are to be and to do. For example, those with a more traditional view expect the pastor to be their primary caregiver in the congregation (e.g., to visit them in the hospital — and possibly in their homes — when they're ill) and to preach well. They expect worship to feature the great Christian music of history. People with the more transformational view will see themselves as sent to ministry; they will expect a less personal relationship with the pastor but deeper relationships with other believers in the congregation (e.g., in their small group). The transitional pastor will find himself or herself ministering to people according to their differing expectations and needs while continuing to lift the transformational vision before the congregation and showing honor to the people and programs that have been significant in the ministry of the church.

For example, there are those in the congregation I serve who feel that the church is paying attention to them only if I, as the senior pastor, visit them. Others are bolstered by the visits and encouragement of fellow church members and see my presence as no more or less helpful than the ministry of their friends in Christ. In such a transitional setting, I serve people according to their diverse expectations while continuing to hold up the vision of a transformational ministry as we continue to lead people from a traditional to a transformational understanding of ministry.

Transitional congregations often have programming from both the traditional approach (a traditional worship service and standard programs for men and women) and the transformational approach (a traditional, blended, and/or contemporary worship service, various kinds of small groups, a variety of ministry teams, and an emphasis on ministry as a lifestyle and not merely a program). As the transition develops, more and more people shift from traditional to transformational expectations of the pastoral staff and ministry programming. This transition may develop in a few years, or it may take a decade or longer. Any transitional congregation must answer the challenge to show honor — *to bless* — traditional ministry programs that have involved a number of members for many years (often for decades), and at the same time *to add* that vision for ministry that will address the changing needs of people with the unchanging Good News of Jesus Christ.

The ministry shifts that I will describe move a traditional ministry into transition and toward transformation. The process of transition can be exceptionally demanding. Introducing change, even change for the right reasons and with worthy goals, can be threatening to those who have invested their lives in their present approach to congregational ministry. Transition here means, in essence, that a new congregation grows within the existing one. Transition should be introduced in such a way that all participants know they are valued, their concerns are heard, and their needs are addressed. And it should be done in such a way that as many people as possible give one another the freedom to do ministry differently within the same congregation. This takes good judgment (what changes to introduce and when, when to hold back, whom to involve), great patience, faith, and perseverance, and *the capacity both to bless what exists now and to add the new.* Since some conflict is inevitable, transition requires leaders (both pastors and members who lead) who have a sound understanding of change management — the guiding principles and practices by which an organization makes the transitions to new behaviors. They will need excellent people skills, and thick skins! Few churches are 100 percent traditional, transitional, or transformational. Every congregation evolves as a dynamic mix of ministry activity and the personal style of its leaders. In a sense, every vital congregation in transition seeks to affirm the things that have blessed participants in the past while adding those new things that are necessary to address the shifting needs and expectations of people with the truth of the Gospel.

Consider the direction in which you believe your own congregation should move, and then, prayerfully and deliberately, take courage, trust God, and work with others to move on. True transformation always comes from the work of the Holy Spirit. It is important to remember that transitional ministry places extra demands on the pastor(s) and other congregational leaders, who often discover many competing expectations and demands in addition to the normal requirements of ministry. Essential to transition is a supportive ruling board that shares the responsibility for change and offers a supportive spirit and excellent judgment as new initiatives develop.

So, what are the elements of a vital vision for ministry? What has to occur to make the transformational church a present reality? In the next several chapters I will outline a number of essential shifts that must take place if we are to move our congregations from their present traditional posture into the transformational posture. One reminder: church vitality has nothing to do with congregational size. As Christ himself reminded us, "Where two or three are gathered in my name, there am I in the midst of them." Every church is a whole church because Jesus Christ is present. Therefore, any church, however big or small, may be a transformational church by God's grace.

CHAPTER THREE

Shifts concerning Vision and Expectation

Beginning with this chapter we will start to look at some of the twelve dynamic shifts necessary to move a congregation in the direction of transformational ministry. Each shift is important and deserves consideration. These are by no means the only shifts or areas of concern for a congregation interested in transition, but they are all critical shifts. (For an excellent treatment of related matters, read Kennon Callahan's *Twelve Keys to an Effective Church*.) As you reflect on each of these shifts, weigh the positive aspects and try to envision each shift in your congregation. What would it look like? Who would be affected? What benefits would you receive? What obstacles would you face? And how would you deal with these?

After each definition of a shift, I have listed several questions. Some are personal, and others are more congregational in focus. I would encourage you to jot down your answers to the questions and your reflections on the material — and have the members of your leadership groups do so as well. Your church will receive maximum benefit if you discuss these questions in your leadership groups.

The first three shifts have to do with the vision you have for your congregation, what you "see" it becoming and doing, and with the expectation you have that your church can indeed become transformational. How you picture that future has a great deal to do with what will happen by God's grace. Imagine your church as a vibrant, transformational fellowship that pulses with life and energy. How would it look? How would it feel?

----

1. Shift from your present hopes for your congregation's future to the high expectation that God has a vital future for your church.

Today's churches frequently demonstrate little genuine excitement about the future, mostly because they are oriented to the past. The transformational church will expect God to act in fresh ways to inspire discipleship and meet the needs of people. "*See, I am doing a new thing!* Now it springs up; do you not perceive it? I am making a way in the desert and streams in the wasteland" (Isa. 43:19, italics added).

Soon after moving to Pittsburgh and becoming pastor of the Pleasant Hills Church, I attended a sack-lunch gathering with a few other pastors in the neighborhood. As the new kid on the block, I was eager to meet my colleagues and to get a better sense of some of the ministry issues for congregations in that part of the city. Imagine my surprise when the discussion question of the day was "How do we assist one another as our churches die?" I learned that there had been a population decrease in the area. Most of the congregations were experiencing slowly diminishing memberships, and many of the programs they provided, from adult choirs to youth ministries, were harder and harder to sustain.

25

"How many people live within a fifteen- to twenty-minute radius?" I asked.

"Oh," they replied, "perhaps 150,000 to 200,000."

What a large number of people! Obviously, the problem wasn't the availability of potential participants in the lives of those congregations. At some point, these congregations had moved away from ministries that inspired people in their Christian faith and effectively spoke to their personal needs. Their problem wasn't a "market problem" — too few people — but the need for new ideas and energy. Our vision for the future can easily diminish when the momentum of our congregation has been decreasing for a long time, and when we lack vision, we tend to focus on the past and how great things were then. If we lack vision, we can only remember the past.

Whatever the current circumstances of your congregation, consider this: *God has a vital future for your church.* Numerical growth may be one measure of church vitality. But the critical measure of vitality is the growth of discipleship and the sensitivity with which people's needs are addressed. Vitality has nothing to do with size. It has everything to do with life and ministry.

I remember when my friend and mentor Jim Tozer began to lead the renewal of the Covenant Presbyterian Church of West Lafayette, Indiana. He began to speak constantly of the "new spirit" in the church. He did this at a time when a committed core of members were seized with a new vision for what God could do in that congregation, but when the majority of members had little clue about the new thing that was happening. But their ears began to perk up when the idea registered with them that something new and wonderful was occurring in their midst. The expectation that God was doing something new inspired the majority of the congregation to begin to look forward to great things.

As Sam Calian, president of Pittsburgh Theological Seminary, puts it, "Building a visionary church is an invitation . . . to all members to take ownership in the enterprise."[1] Picture a transformational future for your church and hold up that vision of vitality to your church. Develop the expectation in the congregation that God is up to something both new and wonderful. Ask God for the guidance you need to cooperate with the work of the Holy Spirit in bringing about this vitality. Remember, ministry begins as an act of faith in God. Ask God to renew your faith, to transform your church, and to use you to help build the spiritual lives of many others.

QUESTIONS FOR REFLECTION AND DISCUSSION

1. What is *your congregation's* attitude? Are they positive, forward-looking, hopeful, anticipating growth in vitality? Or are they downbeat, with a frustrated sense of steady loss and dim prospects for the future? Describe your congregation's attitude.

2. What is *your* attitude toward your church's future? Are you upbeat, looking for new things? Or are you discouraged, and is your language a bit negative? Describe your attitude.

3. Do you believe that the vitality of the church is the work of God? Are you willing to trust God genuinely and to dream the dreams and take the steps (and the risks) that God will lead you to take to bring about vitality in your congregation?

4. Developing a vital church will require learning the princi-

---

1. Calian, *Survival or Revival: Ten Keys to Church Vitality* (Louisville: Westminster John Knox Press, 1998), p. 12.

ples of church vitality, having the faith and the courage to apply them, and giving them the needed priority of time and effort. Is this something you're willing to commit yourself to personally? Are you willing to make this commitment as a governing body or a leadership team?

Supporting Scripture

"Have I not commanded you? Be strong and courageous. Do not be terrified; do not be discouraged, for the LORD your God will be with you wherever you go." (Joshua 1:9)

"I do not consider myself yet to have taken hold of it. But one thing I do: Forgetting what is behind and straining toward what is ahead, I press on toward the goal to win the prize for which God has called me heavenward in Christ Jesus." (Philippians 3:13-14)

----
2. Shift from merely running programs to implementing a vision for ministry.

Today's church frequently uses a program model for ministry. The transformational church begins with vision and creates and modifies ministry initiatives to support its vision (its purpose, the principles of ministry, and the needs of the people it serves).

The Pleasant Hills Church in Pittsburgh, where I have served for a number of years now, has enjoyed a healthy ministry for decades, with good leadership and people who have had a positive spirit. However, when I arrived in the late eighties, I discovered that the congregation exhibited the classic hallmarks of decline, like many denominational churches over the last forty years or so. The congregation had decreased in size, the members had grown older, the facilities had begun to show considerable wear, and the same programs were being recycled year after year. Not surprisingly, all of the stories people told about the church were stories of previous pastors, people, and programs. No stories depicted a different and vital future. As a matter of fact, when I asked people for their vision for the church, they answered, "We want to be like we used to be." The past was their vision for the future. For a vital future, we need dreams and visions that picture a new and transformational church.

What did we do? We blessed and honored the congregation's past and also pictured a different but vibrant future. If we had said things like, "The future doesn't look promising" or "We've lost steam," we would not have valued the contributions of former members and pastors. We had to honor the past and build toward the future. And we started down that path.

Nevertheless, after the first four intense years of working to move the church's vision and program in the direction of the transformational church, I was frustrated and exhausted. I didn't see much real change. When I visited the national assembly meeting of my denomination that year, I bumped into Kirk Hudson, my predecessor's predecessor as pastor of Pleasant Hills.

"Kirk, may I meet you for breakfast?" I asked. "I need your advice." He was happy to agree.

When we met the next morning, I explained the problem. "Kirk, we have worked to bless the traditions of the church and simultaneously have added a transformational vision for the church that is discipleship-directed and need-responsive. We have adapted the ministry programs to our vision by modifying the worship services, adding small groups, sending adults on short-term mission trips, expanding our ministries of care and adult discipleship, and so on. But we just don't see much change."

Kirk leaned across the table until we were eye to eye, and with a warm smile he said to me, "Young man, you are impatient!" That grabbed my attention! He went on to say that the church had not become what it was in a day, and that new life in the church would need a transformational approach to ministry over a long period of time. He was right on both counts.

I have come to understand that real change in the culture of the congregation, real transformation, will require the application of a consistent vital vision for ministry over several years. I realized that I needed to persist in the vision and trust God to create a new church in the midst of the old one. Vitality comes by grace as we bless the history of our churches and the life investments of a great many people and at the same time begin the long-term application of a vital vision for ministry. Some positive change can come quickly to a congregation whose leaders trust God to help them make key changes in direction; other facets of revitalization require patience.

The *vision for ministry* that we use to shape, design, and modify new ministry programs relies upon the seven foundational concepts that follow.

Seven Vital Signs: Foundations of a Vital Ministry

1. *It is Spirit-driven:* God is the author, the initiator, and the finisher of ministry. All ministry is Spirit-driven and Spirit-given. Trust God to work in people's lives. Trust

the Holy Spirit to work in you and through you. Believe that God will use you in the life of another person or in the life of a group or in some other area of service. Ask God for wisdom and help in your ministry. Give God the credit and honor for the fruit of your work. Take courage. Since it is God who works through you, you are free to take some risks. As William Carey said, "Attempt great things for God; expect great things from God."

2. *It is biblically based:* The basis for ministry is the Word of God (along with the Holy Spirit). Scripture both feeds our souls and tells us the "how" of vital ministry. Growth in personal discipleship and congregational vitality occurs when we keep Scripture at the heart of all we do, teaching and preaching its message, equipping people to apply its truths. Within the Bible we find the "why" of ministry as well as much about the "who," "what," "when," "where," and "how." In Scripture we learn the principles and see the biblical pictures — the methods of how ministry can be accomplished through faith, hope, love, and prayer; teaching, caring, and sending forth; hospitality, small groups, and the shared meal. Base your life and your ministry on the principles and truths you see in Scripture.

3. *It is discipleship-directed:* The first major purpose of ministry is to make disciples, followers of Jesus Christ who are committed to one another and who are sent to serve in the world. We encourage and equip persons to make a faith commitment to Jesus Christ and to grow in Christ's image. We encourage one another to love God and to respond to the work and call of God's Word and Spirit in our lives. The whole of Scripture, rightly interpreted, gives us a full expression of the content of discipleship. The deliberate development of spiritual disci-

plines (best supported in the small-group environment) is one very effective way to grow disciples.

4. *It is need-responsive:* The second major purpose of ministry is to nurture the well-being of people. To enable *shalom,* the well-being of persons, we address physical, emotional, mental, spiritual, and social needs, justice concerns, and needs of institutions and communities. This is basic to living the gospel. We assess the needs of the people to whom we want to minister in order to serve them most effectively. We seek to understand their true condition (and our own) so that we may, in all humility, seek to bring new strength and vitality into their lives. We realize that an individual's needs are often the door through which we are able to introduce him or her to Jesus Christ.

5. *It is "gathered-scattered" attentive:* We work to build the fellowship in its "gathered" state of large and small groups, and we seek to equip all believers for the Christian life and ministry when "scattered" to home, workplace, and community. Effective ministry is both communal and missional as it builds disciples, responds to needs, and sends people to ministry in every venue of life. In its communal aspect, ministry addresses every gathering of God's people — from the small group, committee, ministry team, and serving group to larger ministries and the entire congregation. At the same time, as a missional people, we prepare and send church members to be scattered in mission to the home, the workplace, the community, and the world. It is critically important to design ministry for the gathered state that will best enable Christian life, response, and service in the scattered state. We want to equip people for ministry where they spend the majority of their time.

6. *It is principle-patterned:* Foundational principles for ministry are found in Scripture, and effective ministry is patterned and shaped by these principles. Use of these principles allows us to cooperate with the Holy Spirit's ministry among us. Each of these principles is "defining" in that each principle shapes or defines the specific program of ministry that we put into practice. In a sense, a principle offers a picture of how to go about the practice of vital ministry. Many additional useful principles of practical ministry — what ministry is to do and be in a given situation — are based on experience and observation. Master examples of biblical principles (and thus defining practices) of ministry include the following:

- the principle of witness (communicating the good news about Jesus Christ)
- the principle of prayer (praying for the people being ministered to)
- the principle of *koinonia*-care (having fellowship that grows friendships and addresses needs)
- the principle of the Word (teaching and applying Scripture to life)
- the "with me" principle (including people with you in ministry and in life activities, and showing leadership)
- the "send them" principle (sending people to use their spiritual gifts to minister to others by leading groups as well as initiating interpersonal ministry)

A defining vision shapes the life of the congregation and all of its subordinate activities. Such a defning vision for a transformational ministry may be expressed as "Reach — Grow — Send." This "ministry cycle" is a repeating ministry pattern. We "reach" as we witness to, pray for, care for, impart the Word to, and get involved with those who are uninvolved or uncommitted. We "grow" as we pray for, care for, impart the Word to, and get involved with those growing as disciples. We "send" as we equip and send those with whom we are growing to reach and to "grow" still with others.

This ministry cycle is based on the defining practices of vital ministry, all of which rest upon the foundation of the broader biblical vision for ministry that I describe as the seven vital signs:

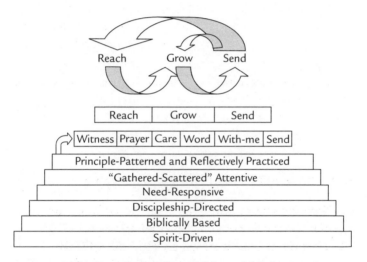

The Foundation for a Vision of Ministry

7. *It is reflectively practiced:* By "reflective" I mean that we don't just "do." We think, we pray, we consider what needs to happen and our role in it, and we appeal to Almighty God for help. Ministry is not merely running a program. Vital ministry means trusting God's Spirit to

change people's lives as we practice principles of ministry. Vital ministry is action that must be preceded by prayerful thought and reflection, the *planning* required to meet needs and effectively employ principles of ministry. Setting aside time for additional reflection during and after a ministry activity or program permits new insights to impact future planning. Schedule deliberate time for prayer and planning — put it on your calendar. Think of prayerful planning as a "spiritual discipline" that will help you consider the needs of people, the principles of ministry, and the appropriate ministry response for yourself personally and for the ministry initiative you are going to design.

Whether you use these seven vital signs or some other biblically grounded vision, in order to grow a transformational church, *you need to have a clear, biblically based vision of what vitality looks like in a congregation and how to go about producing it with God's grace.*

QUESTIONS FOR REFLECTION AND DISCUSSION

1. What present ministries and members of your congregation deserve honor and appreciation?
2. How can you most effectively bless them for the service they have rendered and at the same time secure their blessing for new ministries that will come alongside the present ones? This may involve both public appreciation and personal one-to-one conversation.
3. What vision for ministry do you use? Are you using last year's programs again without carefully and deliberately considering people's present needs? Gathering ideas and attitudes toward ministry that you have received and de-

veloped yourself? Using the seven vital signs described previously? Current authors such as Kennon Callahan *(Twelve Keys to an Effective Church)*, Rick Warren *(The Purpose-Driven Church)*, and William Easum and Thomas Bandy *(Growing Spiritual Redwoods)* also offer biblically grounded visions for a transformational church. (More titles are listed in the back of the book under "Resources for a Transformational Ministry.") You need to have a clear vision of what constitutes vitality in a church in order to develop the ministry necessary to grow that vitality.

Supporting Scripture

"Meanwhile a Jew named Apollos, a native of Alexandria, came to Ephesus. He was a learned man, with a thorough knowledge of the Scriptures. He had been instructed in the way of the Lord, and he spoke with great fervor and taught about Jesus accurately, though he knew only the baptism of John. He began to speak boldly in the synagogue. When Priscilla and Aquila heard him, they invited him to their home and explained to him the way of God more adequately. When Apollos wanted to go to Achaia, the brothers encouraged him and wrote to the disciples there to welcome him. On arriving, he was a great help to those who by grace had believed." (Acts 18:24-27)

"And Jesus came and said to them, 'All authority in heaven and on earth has been given to me. Go therefore and make disciples of all nations, baptizing them in the name of the Father and of the Son and of the Holy Spirit, and teaching them to obey everything that I have commanded you. And remember, I am with you always, to the end of the age.'" (Matthew 28:18-20, NRSV)

----

3. Shift from a maintenance mentality to a sustaining and advancing vision.

Today's church frequently uses last year's programs over again. The transformational church will both sustain present programs and advance with new ministry in accord with the mandates of Scripture and the needs of people.

Even when our programs no longer produce genuine discipleship or effectively facilitate loving relationships, and even though the needs and lifestyles of people have dramatically changed over the last few decades, for the most part the mainline church runs the very same programs with the same organization and the same philosophy it used forty years ago. The culture has not suddenly become hostile to the church; rather, the church is no longer responding to people's present needs. If there is any single common characteristic of typical mainline congregations, it is repetition of last year's programs. Mindless repetition can easily trap us in yesterday's ministry.

Paul Mundey provides an interesting commentary on this point in *Unlocking Church Doors: Ten Keys to Positive Change.* He describes one of the experiments of scientist Jean-Henri Fabre, who placed a number of caterpillars end to end around the rim of a large flowerpot. As he put the caterpillars on the pot, each with its head pushing snugly against the rear of the caterpillar in front of it, they began slowly moving around and around. Fabre thought they'd tire of it, or at least stop for nourishment — but they didn't. Mundey explains what happened: "Through force of habit, the living, creeping circle kept its accustomed pattern for seven days and nights. Only exhaustion and starvation interrupted the larvae's relentless routine. Fabre had placed an ample supply of food just inches from the flowerpot. But the caterpillars were required to leave their familiar circle to eat it. Stuck in the same old routine, bound by the beaten path, they chose not to reach out for an obvious source of life."[2] Does this depict many of our ministries?

I once attended the fortieth-anniversary celebration of a congregation's ministry to women. I noticed that the women's ministries program booklets for each of the forty years were on display, from the first booklet to the last. I picked up the most recent booklet and walked it down the table to compare it with the first booklet. As you probably would guess, the last booklet was in the very same format and described the very same program as the booklet published forty years earlier. It was no surprise that the average participants in the women's ministries on this fortieth anniversary were senior citizens. Working women and women with young children were unable to access the program offerings. Thankfully, in recent years, the women leading that fellowship found a way to bless the elements of the women's organization that were important to long-term participants and to add new ministry groups more suitable for and accessible to younger women and working women of all ages.

If today's church is to move in the direction of transformational ministry, it must shift from maintaining the status quo to *sustaining* with excellence that which is effective and *advancing* new ministry. At Pleasant Hills Church, we have found the basic philosophy of "bless and add" to be very useful. Bless the old; add the new. Honor the past; embrace the future. Bless those elements of program

2. Mundey, *Unlocking Church Doors: Ten Keys to Positive Change* (Nashville: Abingdon Press, 1997), p. 13.

and service that have encouraged and continue to encourage people, while at the same time adding new elements of ministry that will reach other groups of people.

Sometimes, of course, the most appropriate action is to end the old and bring a long-standing ministry to a close. Such a move requires tact and forethought so that those who have invested much of themselves in the ministry see their work being appreciated and honored, not simply wiped out. Sometimes it is easier to bless an existing (although no longer very effective) ministry and add the new one alongside, thus giving honor to both. To advance with new ministry means that the current congregational leadership will either have to work harder or learn to delegate certain kinds of ministry to others who have the interest and the capacity to serve. Significantly, many people in our traditional congregations do not serve today simply because our standard programs bore them. Offer a new and advancing vision, and trust God to raise up additional leadership. "Ask the Lord of the harvest, therefore, to send out workers into his harvest field" (Matt. 9:38).

A final note: Sometimes those in smaller congregations say there aren't enough people to run the ministries they currently have — much less new ministries. But it is amazing how resources and people follow new vision. Frequently congregations have uninvolved people who are willing and eager to serve; they just don't want to invest themselves in the current programs. They are waiting for a new vision, and they will respond to it.

QUESTIONS FOR REFLECTION AND DISCUSSION

1. Which of your present ministries reflect the routine repetition of existing programs?

2. Which of your ministries and programs do you want to sustain with excellence?
3. What new ministry initiatives would meet the needs of people, provide new points for entry and involvement, and build disciples? Develop a list. Then focus on implementing one to three of these initiatives with ministry teams in the next year.
4. Who are the people who can offer leadership to new ministry programs?

Supporting Scripture

"See, I am doing a new thing! Now it springs up; do you not perceive it? I am making a way in the desert and streams in the wasteland." (Isaiah 43:19)

"Since, then, we have such a hope, we act with great boldness." (2 Corinthians 3:12, NRSV)

"But you will receive power when the Holy Spirit has come upon you; and you will be my witnesses in Jerusalem, in all Judea and Samaria, and to the ends of the earth." (Acts 1:8, NRSV)

CHAPTER FOUR

Shifts concerning Ministry to People

The program mentality of the church frequently leads us to uncritically adopt the programs of other congregations or purchase congregational resources available on the market without shaping those resources so they reflect our own vision for ministry (such as the seven vital signs discussed in shift 2) or address our own people's particular situations and needs. Pastors and congregational leaders often think of ministry primarily in terms of programs, but Jesus never began with programs. He began with people — assessing their needs and then addressing them in some ministry initiative. For example, we read in chapter six of the Gospel of Mark that when Jesus took his disciples on a retreat, a crowd of five thousand people came to him, barging in on him and his plans. He had compassion on them because they were like sheep without a shepherd, and so he adjusted his original program — to go on retreat — and he began to teach them. Later that day when the crowd was hungry, Jesus fed them. He assessed their discipleship needs and their physical needs, and those shaped his ministry accordingly.

We have become so enamored of programs as a gauge of church vitality that we have lost sight of the significance of focusing on the spiritual vitality of *people* — that is, seeing personal discipleship as a primary evidence of the vitality of our congregation, and effectively reaching out to the people in our communities. Of course, "programs" — organized ministry initiatives — certainly have a very significant role in transformational ministry when they are made the deliberate means of meeting genuine human needs and helping people grow — really grow — in discipleship. But in the three dynamic shifts we consider in this chapter (shifts 4 through 6 of the 12), our primary concern is *people* — what it takes to make people feel welcome, for people to be developed as genuine disciples of Jesus and sent into the world as God's messengers, and for ministry to be geared to the people outside the church as well as those inside it.

----

4. Shift from an emphasis on friendliness to a ministry of friendliness and hospitality.

Today's church frequently claims to be friendly. The transformational church will offer the gifts of both friendliness and hospitality to all persons.

Friendliness and hospitality are quite different, you know. Suppose you meet me in the fellowship hall and say, "Hi, Stan. How are things going for you? How are the kids? How's the cat? How's the car? Well, I have to be going. It was great talking to you. See you!" That's friendliness — being warm, sociable, and pleasant. All of us like to think of ourselves as friendly people and our churches as friendly congregations.

Hospitality, on the other hand, is quite different from friendliness. Friendliness says, "Hi, how are you?" Hospitality says, "Come into my life!" Hospitality says, "Let's do something together — come over to my house, attend this event with me, join me for a cup of coffee." In church ministry, hospitality says, "Come with me to my fellowship group." It may mean "Come on over to my home," or "We're going to grab a bite to eat — please come with us."

I once met with the elders of a rural church to talk about issues regarding church vitality. They earnestly declared that everyone was welcome to attend their church meetings, from worship services to Sunday school classes. But I suggested that if they really wanted new people to join them, they would need to practice hospitality on a personal basis — that they would have to include those new people not only in their programs but also in their own personal lives.

Afterward, when I was walking out to my car in the parking lot, one of the elders in the church, a woman in her forties, approached me and said, "Stan, in our church there are four couples my age. Every year we spend a week skiing in Colorado. Recently a new couple who is our age began visiting the church. Are you saying we need to include them in our skiing trip? We're a very tight-knit group." I could certainly sense how she wanted me to answer the question! Instead I replied, "I can't say whether or not you should invite them to Colorado. But I can say that they will remain in your church only if you find a way to include them in your personal web of friendships." Six months later I heard that the couple the elder mentioned had left that church. The transformational church will find ways to be both friendly and hospitable.

QUESTIONS FOR REFLECTION AND DISCUSSION

1. How do new people perceive your church? Are you friendly to them? The issue is not whether you are friendly to each other but whether you are friendly to guests.
2. Are you hospitable as a congregation? First, are new participants welcome — truly welcome — in your meetings and gatherings? What evidence do you have that you are or are not receiving new people into your groups?
3. Are you practicing hospitality personally? In your own lives do you (or a fair number of you) regularly include new church members and participants in the activities and gatherings of your personal lives? How can your church more effectively practice hospitality?
4. When is the last time you made a new friend (a close personal friend) of someone you met at church? How can you more effectively practice hospitality?

Supporting Scripture
"Share with God's people who are in need. Practice hospitality." (Romans 12:13)

"Offer hospitality to one another without grumbling." (1 Peter 4:9)

"Do not neglect to show hospitality to strangers, for by doing that some have entertained angels without knowing it." (Hebrews 13:2, NRSV)

----

5. Shift from assuming discipleship to developing discipleship.

Today's church frequently assumes discipleship. The transformational church will lovingly and intentionally develop discipleship in its participants.

I remember going to a dinner meeting of a church fellowship group. After dinner, the program for the night was titled "Latest Developments at General Electric." Well, I was interested in what was going on at G.E., but I doubt that many people that evening received any new motivation to grow in their love for God or care for others. The program of another fellowship group that week featured a person portraying Dolly Madison in a page out of U.S. history. Again we watched an interesting presentation, but I don't think it did much to enhance our discipleship. We so easily assume that people are devout disciples in today's church. When we assume that everyone's faith is mature, then the fellowship groups in the congregation can become little more than social groups.

Perhaps it was once appropriate to assume discipleship was the central focus of our church members. I must say I have been truly astonished by the number of eighty- and ninety-year-olds I have met who have the most wonderful, winsome faith in Jesus Christ and Christian spirituality. However, their children and grandchildren often don't share the vitality of their faith. This kind of "degeneration of faith," as we might call it, is — sadly — not atypical. It shows that we can no longer assume that the people attending our programs are devout followers of Jesus Christ.

On the other hand, there is a remarkable desire among

churched people to grow as authentic followers of Jesus Christ. In 1995, when Ben Johnson, Professor of Christian Spirituality at Columbia Theological Seminary in Decatur, Georgia, began a Certificate in Spiritual Formation program, the response was tremendous — and remains so. People want to grow as disciples and are eager for the leadership and instruction necessary for it to happen.

At Pleasant Hills Church, we have found it helpful to have a written profile of discipleship. The profile we use includes seven basic spiritual disciplines that we use to guide us as we design ministry to help people grow as disciples. I call these disciplines "The Seven Habits of the Burning Heart." The title refers to the seal of John Calvin, which portrays a hand holding a heart that is on fire. Inscribed around the heart are the words "My heart I give to you, O Lord, eagerly and sincerely."

In outline form, the Seven Habits of the Burning Heart are as follows:

1. The habit of devotion (growing in one's relationship with Jesus Christ through worship and the devotional life)
2. The habit of well-being (seeking physical, emotional, and spiritual health)
3. The habit of building family and friendships (building relationships within families and among friends)
4. The habit of fellowship (spending time with other Christians and the small group)
5. The habit of stewardship (managing one's money, sexuality, power, time, and speech)
6. The habit of ministry and mission (nurturing other people in well-being and discipleship)

7. The habit of work (offering my work to God and standing up for God in all situations)[1]

There are many excellent tools available today to help us in spiritual formation: people can grow spiritually by means of wonderful resource materials, small groups, and the deliberate practice of spiritual disciplines. Be alert to the many resources now available for growing disciples and enhancing disciplehip and use them. But remember too that it is not the tools of ministry per se but the work of God's Spirit among us that forms Christ within us. Ask God to grow your congregation into a family of vital, loving disciples of Jesus Christ, and make plans with this vision in mind.

QUESTIONS FOR REFLECTION AND DISCUSSION

1. Does your congregation have a deliberate strategy for building discipleship, or do you assume it will happen through each person's involvement in the church's ongoing programs?
2. Is your congregation building disciples?
3. Do you have a written profile of discipleship that describes key elements of discipleship that you hope to see grow in the life of your people, and do you assess spiritual growth in relation to that profile?
4. What discipleship-building materials are you aware of? Which ones are you using, and which ones will you plan to use?

1. E. Stanley Ott, *Vision for a Vital Church* (Pittsburgh: vitalfaithresources.com, 1994), pp. 15-16. For another profile of discipleship, see the excellent work by Richard Foster entitled *Celebration of Discipline: The Path to Spiritual Growth* (New York: Harper & Row, 1978).

Supporting Scripture

"Then Jesus came to them and said, 'All authority in heaven and on earth has been given to me. Therefore go and make disciples of all nations, baptizing them in the name of the Father and of the Son and of the Holy Spirit, and teaching them to obey everything I have commanded you. And surely I will be with you always, to the very end of the age.'" (Matthew 28:18-20)

"We proclaim him, admonishing and teaching everyone with all wisdom, so that we may present everyone perfect in Christ." (Colossians 1:28)

Paul: "When I remember you in my prayers, I always thank my God. . . . I pray that the sharing of your faith may become effective when you perceive all the good that we may do for Christ." (Philemon 4, 6, NRSV)

----

6. Shift from a primary emphasis on the communal life of the church to a balanced emphasis on the communal and missional life of the church.

Today's church frequently emphasizes the communal state of the church as it gathers for programs and meetings, usually held in the church building and geared to the present participants. The transformational church will balance its communal and missional emphasis with ministry in the gathered state and in the scattered state (home, community, and workplace).

Typically, most of our planning for church activities centers on preparation for various gatherings of church people. However, the vast majority of the active members of our churches spend less than 5 percent of their time in the church buildings. Members live their lives primarily at home, in the workplace, in their community, and in the world. A transformational church not only instructs and inspires its members in its gatherings to study the apostles' teaching and share in fellowship, breaking of bread, and prayers (Acts 2:42), but also equips its members to scatter into their worlds as literal representatives of Jesus Christ.

What we need to recover is an ancient truth. The church is by nature both communal (*ekklesia* — the assembly of called-out ones) and missional (*missio Dei* — the mission of God). So we read in Mark 3:14, "He [Jesus] appointed twelve . . . that they might be *with* him and that he might *send* them out to preach" (emphasis added). Communal and missional — "with" and "send." We see the communal emphasis in Matthew 11:28: "Come to me, all you who are weary and burdened, and I will give you rest." And we see the missional emphasis in John 20:21: "As the Father has sent me, I am sending you."

The vast majority of church programming is centered on the communal aspect, with invitations issued to churched people: "Come to our worship service. Come to our women's circle, our youth group, our special gathering." We have done a good job of teaching people to attend programs and to listen. The down side is that over the last generation or two, congregations became fixated on their own internal programs to the exclusion of serious engagement with the culture. Very little of what we might call typical church programming intentionally works to reach people who are outside of the church. And the church's loss of clear missional vision came at the very moment that the church was losing its position at the center of American culture. As a result, congregational programs increasingly fail to address the needs and concerns of their present participants, while continuing to use language (words, symbols, media) no longer used or understood in the wider culture.[2]

The transformational congregation deliberately prepares its people to "go into the world" and to "reach people for Christ and lead them into the church." Such congregations design their various programs and activities to speak to those who are on the "outside" as well as those who are on the "inside." One practical means of simultaneously addressing the needs of people while attending to both the communal and the missional facets of ministry is the use of of the ministry cycle "Reach — Grow — Send." We seek to "reach" people, welcoming them into our fellowship and introducing them to faith in Christ; we work to help them "grow" in personal discipleship; and we "send" them to ministry and leadership. In many congregational ministries, the majority (or the entirety) of planning is directed to "grow" those already involved, with little thought or planning given to involving more people and developing new leadership among the present participants.

How can this ministry cycle be implemented? "Reach — Grow — Send" are three stages in the "Relational Highway," a term coined by Scott Stevens to describe the basic philosophy of the Crossover Ministries he directs at Pleasant Hills Church. The "reach" program, which involves several hun-

---

2. For an extensive treatment of this, see Darrell L. Guder et al., *Missional Church* (Grand Rapids: Eerdmans, 1998); Leonard Sweet, *Post-Modern Pilgrims* (Nashville: Broadman & Holman, 2000); and Brian D. McLaren, *The Church on the Other Side: Doing Ministry in the Post-Modern Matrix* (Grand Rapids: Zondervan, 1998).

dred young people every week, provides a variety of fun, interesting, yet spiritually compelling activities designed to attract students with a minimal level of Christian experience. Students involved in the "reach" events eventually move into the "grow" stage, in which they receive teaching and encouragement in a wide variety of the aspects of Christian faith and practice through classes, small groups, and mentoring. Finally, in the "send" stage, the students are "sent" — deployed in leadership and ministry to those in the "reach" and "grow" stages. By focusing on how to win the seekers and the uninvolved students while simultaneously providing fellowship-growth events and engaging students in the conduct of ministry and leadership, the overall ministry remains consciously missional and communal.[3]

Virtually any congregational ministry involving groups of people — from the worship service to ministries for men, women, children, and youth — may use the "Reach — Grow — Send" pattern in order to be more simultaneously communal and missional. To be effective with the "reach" stage, ministries will have to shift from simply repeating last year's programs to carefully considering the needs and interests of the people they want to reach, and then organizing accordingly. Some "reach" events and emphases will be planned to draw newcomers and seekers. They provide a means of involving new people and a way of offering a clear and winsome witness. It is important to remember that congregational life is tremendously energized when there is a flow of people who are coming to faith in Jesus Christ. And "reach" ministries help members of the congregation to see the people in their communities with new eyes, and to remember, "I

3. For more information, see the web site address (http://www.crossover-online.com).

am sent, in all humility, by my Lord, to engage in ministry in my home, my workplace, and my community."

QUESTIONS FOR REFLECTION AND DISCUSSION

1. Where are your congregation's people between Sundays? One way to get at this is to make a list of every place that you've been in the last week. If you're making this list in a group, put your lists together. Add the total number of places, divide by the number of people in the group, and then multiply times your congregation's membership to get an idea of the incredible range of your congregation's involvement.

2. How are you presently preparing people in practical and specific ways to represent Jesus Christ in the home, the workplace, and the community? Do you have a ministry that helps individual church members discover their specific gifts and then connects them to specific ministries?

3. How might you begin to regularly build "reach" events and emphases into your ministry (whether it is a minstry to men, women, children, youth, or people of all ages) instead of concentrating only on those activities whose intent is to "grow" the present participants?

4. How will you develop a sense of "sent-ness" in your people, that they may see themselves as sent by God, in all humility, to serve those around them wherever they may be, in the name of Christ?

Supporting Scripture

"He appointed twelve — designating them apostles — that they might be with him and that he might send them out to preach." (Mark 3:14)

"Therefore go and make disciples of all nations, baptizing them in the name of of the Father and of the Son and of the Holy Spirit, and teaching them to obey everything I have commanded you. And surely I will be with you always, to the very end of the age." (Matthew 28:19-20)

CHAPTER FIVE

Shifts concerning Congregational Program

It is remarkably easy for the traditional congregation to "run last year's program over again" rather than to implement a new vision for ministry. I know this from my own experience. At one point I reviewed about twenty years of the congregation's programs for men, women, and children. As I looked over the records, I realized that the form and substance of those programs remained essentially unaltered for twenty to forty years. There were few changes other than the names of people in various leadership positions. It dawned on me then that while we had a clear and grand vision for the future, in practice we were merely repeating the same routine year after year — a congregational version of the movie *Groundhog Day*. Our real vision was to maintain. We were running in place (stuck in the present because we were repeating the past). As George Odiorne puts it, "Most people get caught in the Activity Trap! They become so enmeshed in activity they lose sight of why they are doing it, and the activity becomes a false goal, an end in itself. Successful people never lose sight of their goals, the hoped-for outputs."[1] Activity — and certainly

---

1. Odiorne, *Management and the Activity Trap* (New York: Harper & Row, 1974), p. 6.

church activity — that is repeated year after year without change easily gets out of step with the current needs of people we want to serve and the vision of the ministry. Transformational ministries deliberately *think* about these things in times of planning, of thinking ahead, and make the adjustments necessary to effectively meet human needs and to grow disciples on an ongoing basis.

The three dynamic shifts discussed in this chapter (shifts 7 through 9 out of 12) address some of the areas of congregational program and practice that are potentially most resistant to change. Yet they also have the potential to bear bountiful fruit in individual life-change and to encourage the worship life and the group life of the congregation.

----

7. Shift from an unchanging worship format to a ministry of worship and music responsive to the variety of needs present in the congregation and in the community you want to reach.

Today's church frequently worships in a traditional way. The transformational church will blend the great worship and sacred music of history with new expressions of worship and music. It will find ways to keep the worship experience fresh and alive while sustaining the essential worship distinctions of the denomination or communion of which the congregation is a part.

A few years ago I happened to see the comedy movie *Sister Act* in New Orleans. Whoopi Goldberg stars as a slightly shady lounge singer whose life is in danger. Some Catholic nuns hide her in their convent, and she begins a revival in their worship experience by bringing in sixties "oldies" music rewritten as "hymns with a beat." Halfway through the movie, my wife leaned over and whispered, "Why aren't you laughing?" I answered, "This is serious business!" I could hear the people around me laughing and whispering to one another, "If church music would sound like this, then I'd go." I grew up as a Baby Boomer with the Beatles and with "oldies" music. I realized that if I could attend a church with upbeat music like that, I'd go too! At the same time, many Boomers — indeed, people of all ages — prefer more traditional music. We find ourselves in a time with an amazing range of both musical preferences and musical possibilities.

Worship transition today is one of the most challenging arenas of change — and potentially the toughest one — facing the mainline church. I knew that if we turned the traditional worship service at Pleasant Hills Church into a "sister act" without first considering the music preferences of the people we serve, I'd be standing in the unemployment line. Although many of our present members, as well as the people we wanted to reach, loved contemporary music, many other current members were attached to the traditional music they had always heard in church. We realized that we had to find a way to "bless and add" — to continue to offer with approval the great sacred music of the past and at the same time introduce the great music of today. We wanted — and still strive today — to touch as many people as possible with our music and worship, knowing that, given the diversity of today's musical tastes and styles, we cannot please everyone. Worship is an art form, and therefore the response to it is subjective. Each of us likes what we like.

Many congregations are experimenting with new worship formats today. In our case, we slowly shifted both of our traditional services into the blended format and eventually shifted one of those into a more contemporary format. Many congregations are adding contemporary or "Gen X" services on Sunday morning, before or after the traditional service. Some congregations are offering more contemporary services at night — sometimes on a Saturday evening. There doesn't seem to be a single correct pattern, though perhaps in time clearer patterns will emerge.

Worship transition will happen when the pastor and the minister of music, along with other key leaders, begin to ask, "How can our worship service best speak to the variety of needs present in the congregation and in the community of unchurched we want to reach?" There are many excellent books and resources available on worship and music transition. Use them as you seek a worship style or styles that will lead your church into the future while showing honor to the worship forms and elements that have helped people worship in the past. Adding a new worship service places significant additional demands on the pastoral staff and those involved in worship support. One of the issues to ponder when deciding whether to add a new service or to change the style of an existing one is how much time and energy your pastoral staff can devote to this change. Do what you can do without exhausting people or causing burnout. In this regard I believe you will find *Contemporary Worship in the Reformed Tradition* by David A. Miller very helpful.[2]

True worship by any congregation is the work of God's Spirit, not simply certain music selections or a particular order of worship. Changing worship style is not a simple or an automatic solution to revitalizing a church. It is simply one factor to consider if the people you want to reach have some-

2. Miller, *Contemporary Worship in the Reformed Tradition* (Pittsburgh: Vital Faith Resources, 2001).

what different preferences from the people you currently serve. However, if changing worship style and format is sure to lead to excessive conflict, or if adding another worship service will overtax the present pastoral and music staff, then bless your worship service as it is, making perhaps a few minor shifts in worship style and music. Add vitality by first making some of the other shifts described in this book.

QUESTIONS FOR REFLECTION AND DISCUSSION

1. Is your worship service the same in format, music, style, and "feel" as it was ten years ago? Twenty? Thirty?
2. What are the preferences of the people you want to serve with your worship service(s), including those already inside the church and those lesser churched who live in the community?
3. What issues would you have to resolve to shift the style of a present worship service or add a new one?

Supporting Scripture

"The trumpeters and singers joined in unison, as with one voice, to give praise and thanks to the LORD. Accompanied by trumpets, cymbals and other instruments, they raised their voices in praise to the LORD and sang: 'He is good; his love endures forever.' Then the temple of the LORD was filled with a cloud, and the priests could not perform their service because of the cloud, for the glory of the LORD filled the temple of God." (2 Chronicles 5:13-14)

"Praise the LORD.
Praise God in his sanctuary; praise him in his
mighty heavens.

Praise him for his acts of power; praise him for
his surpassing greatness.
Praise him with the sounding of the trumpet,
praise him with the harp and lyre,
praise him with tambourine and dancing,
praise him with the strings and flute,
praise him with the clash of cymbals, praise him
with resounding cymbals.
Let everything that has breath praise the Lord.
Praise the Lord." (Psalm 150)

"He put a new song in my mouth, a song of praise to our
God." (Psalm 40:3, NRSV)

- -

8. Shift from primarily audience-oriented
programming (e.g., worship services, classes) to a
balance of audience-oriented ministry and face-to-
face ministry (e.g., small groups, one-on-one
spiritual direction).

- -

Today's church runs mostly audience-oriented programs.
The transformational church will balance audience-oriented
programming with face-to-face groups. This is the ministry
principle of "large group–small group balance." Remember
that the early church in Acts gathered in the temple for worship (large group) and in one another's homes (small
groups) for prayer and fellowship.

In the audience-oriented format, one person speaks to
many. This format includes most worship services, women's
circles, men's breakfasts, and Sunday school classes. In the

traditional church, we have taught our members to be receivers of other people's insights and to value the teaching ministry of the church. Certainly the church's teaching ministry is important, because listening to teachers and preachers can enable spiritual growth. However, other ministry formats for prayer and for engaging Scripture, such as the small group, are equally effective means — and in many cases much more effective means — of growth in discipleship. Significant spiritual growth frequently happens when a person in a small group has the opportunity to speak face-to-face about faith and heart-to-heart about personal questions and experiences.

Small groups also add the crucial ingredient of interpersonal relationships to congregational life. People are looking for new, deeper, and more genuine friendships in the church, not merely the opportunity to attend meetings. It is in the face-to-face small group of seven to ten people that individuals are most fully known and deeply loved within the church. In this context, real relationships grow and blossom. Where in your congregation's ministry today can the typically involved person talk regularly with other believers on a "face-to-face" basis about the things of the Spirit? Where can they share the ordinary experiences of their lives with one another and be most present to one another in times of difficulty? The most vital congregations of all sizes today are working to center themselves in dynamic worship and in the small-group experience. In this "large group–small group" balance people may best be enabled and encouraged to grow in their relationship with God and with one another.

I think of my friend Dick McCombs, who found excuse after excuse to avoid participating in a small-group Bible study. Years after finally joining such a small group and loving it, growing deeply in his spiritual life and his understanding of Scripture, Dick said to me, "The reason I put off joining a small group was that I didn't want to reveal my ignorance of the Bible." His comment may seem surprising — but this is a common feeling among many longtime church members. Dick had been an active member of the church for forty years, had often served as an elder, had led a variety of ministries, and had chaired pastoral search committees. But simply attending worship and actively participating in various activities didn't give Dick the opportunities to thoroughly understand the content and substance of Scripture. Dick began to grow significantly in his Christian experience when he enjoyed the combination of worship *and* small-group fellowship. In worship each week the preaching and teaching encouraged him. In his small-group Bible study he had the opportunity to speak with others about his own insights into Scripture and to grapple more personally with the implications of those insights for his own life. Large group–small group balance offered him tremendous encouragement and growth in his spiritual life.

I must warn you that with our present emphasis on audience-oriented programming in the traditional church, we have actually taught people to be uneasy about the face-to-face setting. People may fear being asked to share something personal or to pray for another person out loud — or afraid, as Dick was, of revealing what they perceive to be their ignorance about the Bible. Given that conditioning and the busyness of everyday life, small groups are not an easy or automatic development for a traditional church. They take tremendous work to launch and sustain. But the care-giving and faith-nurturing result is so fruitful and powerful in the lives of those involved that it is well worth the effort.

QUESTIONS FOR REFLECTION AND DISCUSSION

1. What is your balance of audience-oriented and face-to-face ministry? Which of your groups offer only one or the other? List them.

2. How can you add a small-group or face-to-face component to existing groups? This may not be appropriate in every group or ministry. On the other hand, some people who gather to hear a speaker or teacher will meet subsequently in small groups. Sometimes face-to-face sharing and reflecting — even praying — can happen in groups of four within the larger group meeting.

3. What strategy will you use to begin a movement of small groups within the life of your congregation? For more on this, see my book entitled *Small Group Life: A Guide for Members and Leaders* (Pittsburgh: vitalfaithresources.com, 1994).

Supporting Scripture

"On another occasion Jesus began to teach by the lake. The crowd that gathered around him was so large that he got into a boat and sat in it out on the lake, while all the people were along the shore at the water's edge. . . . When he was alone, the Twelve and the others around him asked him about the parables." (Mark 4:1, 10)

"Every day they continued to meet together in the temple courts. They broke bread in their homes and ate together with glad and sincere hearts, praising God and enjoying the favor of all the people. And the Lord added to their number daily those who were being saved." (Acts 2:46-47)

"Jesus said, 'For where two or three are gathered in my name, I am there among them.'" (Matthew 18:20, NRSV)

----

9. Shift from adding new people to established groups to adding new groups.

Today's church frequently expects new people to join established groups. The transformational church will grow by sustaining old groups and adding new groups.

Churches rarely grow very much by getting new people to join established groups. Established groups — groups within the life of your congregation that in many cases have existed for years — tend to be stable webs of friendship. They do take in new people, but mostly by adoption, one at a time. Indeed, Carl Dudley, my professor of ministry at McCormick Seminary, used to say that most smaller churches grow by adopting people. People don't join a program; they must enter into the congregation's web of relationships. New groups generated within the life of a congregation offer easy entry points for people to make new friendships and find a place to belong.

I once observed a senior-citizens group that met on a monthly basis for dinner and fellowship. I slowly discovered that although new people were coming into the church, they never stayed in that particular group. Then I realized that whenever that group met, the same people always sat at the same tables — old friends naturally gravitated toward each other. When new people sat at these tables, they unintentionally displaced some regular members. When the visitors eventually figured this out, they knew they were not truly welcome.

In a situation like this, it is better to bless the group as it is rather than berate members for not being more invitational. They only sit with old friends out of love, not out of some malicious intent to shut others out. To welcome new people, it is easier to add new tables — or, better yet, an entirely new fellowship group. New people fit most easily into new groups.

When we were trying to understand the involvement and assimilation patterns of our church participants in our various groups, we approached thirty of the fellowship groups in the church with two questions. First we asked, "Is your group open to new people?" Every single group leader said, "Yes, we're open to new people joining our group." Next we asked, "May we have a look at whatever attendance records you have?" When we reviewed these records, we discovered that while all thirty groups professed to be open to new people, only seven actually took in new people, and the total number of those new participants wasn't particularly significant. We realized that if we shifted our focus from "getting more people" into our existing groups to the creation of entirely new groups, the total number of participants would grow much more rapidly.

This example shows that one of the best straightforward strategies for growing your congregation is to have a clear strategy (a plan and a timeline) for adding new groups. Nearly every congregation can launch at least one new group a year (a Bible-study group, a service-oriented group, a class, a music group). It does require vision and the will to call someone to leadership and send him or her to the task. That "call" may be easier than you might at first think. Even in congregations in which there appears to be a leadership shortage, there are often people waiting on the sidelines who would be eager to lead a new group with a new vision. Two kinds of groups that can contribute very effectively to congregational vitality are small groups and entry-point groups (both discussed in shift number 5).

Let me add a small "p.s." to the matter of getting existing groups to add new people. Remember that the sixth shift involves moving from an emphasis on people involved in the life of the church to an emphasis on the communal and missional life of the church. Most church groups are fixated on the communal aspect of their life — which is why it's easier to get more people involved by adding new groups than by getting groups to add new people. However, in the ongoing transition of your congregation from a traditional to a transformational approach, you will want to progressively lead more and more of your group leaders to embrace the "Reach — Grow — Send" formula. This makes the missional winning of new people to faith in Jesus Christ and to involvement in groups as much a part of their planning process as their current communal emphasis that simply focuses on growing the existing participants as disciples.

QUESTIONS FOR REFLECTION AND DISCUSSION

1. List your present groups. Which ones are genuine entry points, which is demonstrated by the consistent addition of new participants over the last year?

2. What new groups can you add that will provide new points of entry and involvement? Such groups may be small-group Bible studies, other study groups, service groups, ministry teams, and groups based on life stage or life situation, such as groups for couples, singles, working women, working men, mothers of young children, retired people, and so on.

3. There are far more group possibilities than most congregations can implement. But if you launch just one or two new groups a year, in five years you'll have five to ten new groups! Who are your potential leaders? Which ones have

the will and the skill to lead a group, minister to human need, and build Christian discipleship? Remember, you may have potential leaders who are not presently involved simply because they are waiting for new vision.

Supporting Scripture

"No one sews a patch of unshrunk cloth on an old garment, for the patch will pull away from the garment, making the tear worse. Neither do men pour new wine into old wineskins. If they do, the skins will burst, the wine will run out and the wineskins will be ruined. No, they pour new wine into new wineskins, and both are preserved." (Matthew 9:16-17)

"After this the Lord appointed seventy-two others and sent them two by two ahead of him to every town and place where he was about to go. . . . The seventy-two returned with joy and said, 'Lord, even the demons submit to us in your name.'" (Luke 10:1, 17)

CHAPTER SIX

Shifts concerning the Practice of Leadership

In the traditional congregation, leadership is often very hierarchical in nature, with a chain of authority connecting every committee, ministry program, and person to the ruling board. The driving force of such leadership is the desire to maintain control. This is evidenced in a tendency to dwell on policy-making and the review and approval or disapproval of all ministry initiatives within the life of the congregation.

Transformational congregations are far less interested in such micromanagement and are much more interested in setting people free to accomplish ministry and raising up the leaders to do it. They successfully negotiate the balancing act of sound supervision and permission-giving blessing. While accomplishing the work of oversight required by church polity and good leadership, the pastor and boards shift from merely reviewing reports and regulating every detail of church life to considering questions such as "Who has a new idea or a passion for a ministry initiative? How can we connect more people to such a person?" This is a "sending" mentality that grows out of faith rather than a controlling attitude that is rooted in fear.

The three dynamic shifts in this chapter (the final three

of the twelve shifts) address these attitudes and the practices of transformational leadership. They address a huge issue for most congregations — how to generate more people who are willing and able to lead — and the equally vital matter of connecting every single participant with his or her personal ministry.

---

10. Shift from a "leader-deploying" ministry to a "leader-developing" ministry, from committees to ministry teams.

Today's church focuses on deploying the leaders it has. The transformational church will not only deploy current leaders but also seek to develop new leaders.

There is a vast difference between using and developing leaders. A simple example makes the point. Let's say a vibrant young couple begins to attend your church. The very first Sunday they show up, you can practically hear the people sitting around them thinking, "Ah! Our new youth leaders," or "Wonderful! Our new primary teachers," and so on. Clearly the couple are leaders whose apparent gifts the church wants to use. To give leaders who join your church something to do is to deploy those leaders — to deploy them in the truly good sense of giving them a place to serve. To *develop* leaders, on the other hand, is to take a number of people who currently are non-leaders, as well as the present leaders, and help both groups build their leadership skills.

Our society no longer produces leaders the way it once did. Twenty years ago, if you were a twelve-year-old and you wanted to play a game of softball, *you* conceived the vision to play ball, *you* exercised the will and skill to recruit some friends to play, *you* organized the teams, *you* learned to care for your teammates, and *you* played ball. In other words, you had to learn and practice the skills of leadership if you wanted to play ball. Now we put our children on adult-directed teams. The adults put the teams together, assign kids to playing positions, decide who plays when, and so on. The same thing is happening across the range of experiences our children have. We teach them to be "do-ers" rather than leaders. To "grow" them as leaders, we must place them in situations where they must develop the will and learn the skills necessary to lead others to accomplish a shared vision.

Where do people, both young persons and adults, learn to conceive a vision? Where do they learn to have the will and the skill and the courage to recruit other people to accomplish the vision? And where do they learn to care for those they lead? It is time for the church to stop expecting new leaders — people who have already been taught to lead by our society — to show up in new membership classes. It is time for us to *develop* leaders. Small groups develop new leaders; short-term mission teams develop new leaders; ministry leaders who deliberately choose apprentice leaders (not simply assistant leaders) develop new leaders.

Two of the most effective means of growing new leaders are small groups and ministry teams. Small groups typically involve from seven to ten people, although they may be as small as two or three and as large as fourteen. Small groups use a simple meeting pattern: "Word — Share — Prayer." Because they're small enough to permit everyone to speak and because they engage in Bible study, share their blessings and needs with one another, and pray for one another, they experience Christian fellowship *(koinonia)* to a much greater degree than those who merely attend church and various audience-oriented programs. As a result, small-group members grow in both discipleship and leadership and often become leaders within the congregation.

Ministry teams combine the best of the small-group concept with the best of committee life. Such teams, like small groups and committees, typically involve less than a dozen people. By spending time in "Word — Share — Prayer," sharing meals together on a regular basis, and other means of intentionally developing their Christian community, the ministry team fosters some key experiences usually not encountered in committee life — deliberate encouragement of personal discipleship, growth of new personal friendships among team members, and increased passion to accomplish the ministry vision of the team. Like committees, ministry teams assign tasks to members based on interest, experience, and availability. Ministry teams often meet more frequently than the standard monthly committee and put tremendous energy into fulfilling their purpose. The consequence of all this is that ministry teams develop people both as disciples and as leaders at the same time they accomplish their ministry vision.

It is common to discover ministries in established congregations led by one person alone (Sunday school teacher, choir leader, adult Bible class leader). When such people move on, finding new leadership is often a critical matter if no one has been groomed to take over. The ministry-team approach to leading ministries offers the additional benefit of continuity of leadership. The team "grows" people who are ready to step up when they are needed.

You can move your congregation in the direction of team-based ministry by transitioning its present committees to a ministry-team format and by determining to begin all new ministries with ministry teams. Team transition requires some discretion and some simple planning. Discretion is necessary because some committees simply will not want to change from a purely task-oriented format, and others will need to be gently led. Bless those who are reluctant to change and work with those who will. Over time you can invite people who are amenable to the team concept to join standing committees. Meanwhile, devise straightforward plans to introduce a "Word — Share — Prayer" component into the first twenty to thirty minutes of the meetings of willing committees. Interestingly, even if they don't extend their meeting time, they will get their work done! Invite them to break bread together about three times a year — perhaps to conduct their meetings over a meal. Encourage them to do some fun things together designed to develop deeper fellowship among them. With both committees in transition and new ministry teams, use whatever resources are available to you to assign people individual tasks based on their passion for ministry and spiritual gifts. Remember, by God's grace you *can* develop new leaders.

QUESTIONS FOR REFLECTION AND DISCUSSION

1. Is your congregation's pool of leaders growing or shrinking?
2. Where do most of your new leaders come from? From new-member classes? From within the congregation?
3. What will you do to deliberately begin to develop new leaders? Excellent approaches include getting people into small groups and into ministry-team leadership.

Supporting Scripture
"When he had finished praying, Jesus left with his disciples and crossed the Kidron Valley. On the other side

71

there was an olive grove, and he and his disciples went into it. Now Judas, who betrayed him, knew the place, *because Jesus had often met there with his disciples.*" (John 18:1-2, emphasis added)

"Then he said to his disciples, 'The harvest is plentiful but the workers are few. Ask the Lord of the harvest, therefore, to send out workers into his harvest field.'" (Matthew 9:37-38)

"Then Barnabas went to Tarsus to look for Saul, and when he found him, he brought him to Antioch. So for a whole year Barnabas and Saul met with the church and taught great numbers of people. The disciples were first called Christians at Antioch." (Acts 11:25-26)

- -
11. Shift from a controlling leadership to a permission-giving "sending" leadership.
- -

Today's church frequently withholds permission for new ministry. The transformational church will be permission-giving when it comes to new ministry, while at the same time holding to its central purpose and principles.

Church leaders are frequently uptight, permission-withholding, afraid of risk, and unwilling to attempt new or different forms of ministry. Such leaders can become preoccupied with small questions like "Why are the paper-towel dispensers empty?" rather than big issues like "How can we make this or that new ministry idea a reality?" In permission-withholding churches, an acquaintance of mine has joked, "it is easier to receive forgiveness than it is to get permission." Such a church is missing out on so much. A congregation releases huge potential when the staff, elders, deacons, and other leaders trust God, take risks, and "just say yes" to new dreams for ministry. (Thanks to Dick Towner, my good friend, for introducing me to the concept of permission-giving ministry.)[1]

I've learned the importance of permission-giving from firsthand experience. One evening I was strolling through the fellowship hall of my church when I noticed four women sitting at a table with their Bibles open. Assuming they were a small-group Bible study intent on their discussion, I began walking past them, but they asked me to stop. It turned out that all of them had been on short-term mission trips that had changed their lives. Now they were brainstorming, trying to think of ways to raise money to send more people on mission trips. They asked me if it would be all right to sell T-shirts to raise money for mission.

Immediately fifty alarm bells went off in my head. I was trained in the "no fund-raisers" school of stewardship. A number of thoughts flashed through my mind, including, "No way are we going to sell T-shirts for mission. People ought to give from heartfelt commitment." Then it hit me: "Stan, what are you thinking about?" Five years ago just a small handful cared about mission in this church. These faithful few would stand up at congregational meetings and protest the inadequate money for missions. Most members of the congregation didn't really care. Then we began to send them on short-term mission trips into the city, to Appalachia

---

1. For an excellent discussion of permission-giving congregations, see William Easum, *Sacred Cows Make Gourmet Burgers* (Nashville: Abingdon Press, 1995).

and other places of need across America, and to Costa Rica and Malawi. Suddenly a lot of us began to care about mission.

Here was a group of women who had the vision to secure the funds to send people on mission trips. No one had asked them to do it, no one had given them permission to do it, and I was thinking of saying No? It was time to be a permission-giver. "Do it," I said to them. "Propose your idea to the mission committee." The committee backed it, the elders backed it, great enthusiasm resulted — and no, it didn't set a terrible fund-raising precedent.

A permission-giving board of elders will establish the defining vision and defining practices of the congregation. The defining vision captures the central purpose of the congregation, which can be expressed in a few sentences, sometimes in a single sentence. Examples of such defining vision include "To know Christ and make Christ known" and "To make disciples." The defining vision of Pleasant Hills Church is "Reach — Grow — Send." Defining practices are "bear witness, love God, build fellowship, grow disciples, develop leaders, and send to ministry." The point of a defining vision is to say to the whole congregation and every program, ministry, and group of the congregation, "This is what we expect you will seek to accomplish while you fulfill whatever other mandates your ministry may have."

Permission-giving leaders also delineate a set of defining traits (e.g., integrity, excellence, enthusiasm, and hospitality) and practices (e.g., such as developing small groups and ministry teams and sharing meals) to be used to shape ministry. With the defining vision and defining traits and practices clearly stated, the permission-giving board then delegates broad authority to the staff and various leadership teams and committees of the congregation. They are saying, in effect, "As long as you seek to accomplish the defining vision, embody the traits, and employ the practices that have been outlined, you have our blessing to pursue the particular vision for ministry that you have. All we ask is that you communicate with us on a regular basis so that we know what's happening." This is the biblical practice of "sending" people to ministry: "Again Jesus said, 'Peace be with you! As the Father has sent me, I am sending you'" (John 20:21).

In effect, the elders are saying to those in a ministry area such as Christian education or adult ministries, "Instead of asking us if it's OK to start a class or men's breakfast or singles group, *just do it*. It rests within your area of ministry initiative. Be sure to hold our congregation's defining vision, traits, and practices in mind in your ministry development, and keep us informed. Let us know if there are legal or funding issues you need us to address. Let us know how it's going." The board can measure every ministry's effectiveness by asking how it is fulfilling the congregation's defining vision and employing its defining practices.

This approach, of course, is based on *trust*. The elders trust leadership teams to use good judgment and initiative in developing new ministries in accordance with the central purpose and principles of the congregation. The various leadership teams in turn trust the elders to support them and to back their visions. If something fails occasionally, so what? Obviously the pastoral staff and other leaders are available to help shape and give direction to those seeking to launch new ministry endeavors. When the elders or members of the governing board use a "sending" philosophy, their function changes from merely setting policy and running programs. The pastor and board now work to support those in the congregation who have ideas for ministry that fulfill the purposes of the congregation. The ministry is no longer limited by the time and energy of the elders and pastors; the ministry now grows at the rate at which people develop vision and discover that their ideas will be supported. Elders' meetings also change. Long business meetings give way to a time of Bible study and prayer followed by brief reports and action designed to endorse the ministry-program initiatives of others within the life of the church.

A recent occurrence in Pleasant Hills Church can serve as an example. When some of us conceived the vision of taking a team on a short-term mission trip, the elders did not spend any time solving the logistical problems involved (money, insurance, training, travel, and so on). They blessed those with the vision to proceed, knowing they would be the best people to solve the problems. In the transformational church, the boards will be less concerned with the details of programming and more concerned with prayerfully discerning ways of equipping and sending and increasing the number of church members who do ministry in their church and community.

One way to think about becoming permission-giving is to think in terms of several "levels" of sending. The lower levels exercise a tighter control, while the higher levels loosen up considerably.

Level 1: We tell you what to do.

Level 2: You ask us what to do.

Level 3: You ask us for permission to do what you want to do.

Level 4: You act on your own but inform us immediately.

Level 5: You act on your own and inform us routinely.

Level 6: You act on your own.[2]

2. For a study of degrees of initiative, see "Management Time: Who's Got the Monkey?" *Harvard Business Review* 52, no. 6 (November-December 1974).

These levels actually illustrate the way we raise children. We use Level 1 through Level 3 when a child is young. As the child becomes more mature, we move to Levels 4 and 5. Finally, when we reach Level 6, the child is ready to leave home. Many traditional ruling boards and leadership groups operate at Level 3: they must give the "okay" for everything. A transformational church operates at Level 5 and Level 6 with many of its ministries. People and ministries are free to initiate within the scope of their responsibilities or vision as long as they adhere to the congregation's central vision. They keep their ruling board or leadership team informed routinely because that board bears ultimate responsibility for the ministry. When the central vision is clear and the leadership of a ministry is mature and trustworthy, then Levels 5 and 6 give people freedom to initiate new vision for ministry. (Levels 3 and 4 would still come into play if a ministry plan has some significant risk associated with it, or if the leadership is inexperienced or in need of additional support.)

The church is to be a grace-full community. In a trusting, permission-giving environment, many wonderful things will be free to happen. In transformational churches with appropriate linkages between the leadership board and ministry teams, a permission-giving philosophy coupled with ministry team-based activity is a powerful combination. The board continues to provide the boundaries and guidance required of sound leadership while simultaneously "sending" teams to initiate new congregational ministry. Become permission-givers, "senders," and blessers of the ministry ideas that God gives the people in your church.

QUESTIONS FOR REFLECTION AND DISCUSSION

1. When your ruling board, leaders, and committees meet, is the basic attitude one of blessing new ideas ("Do it — just keep us informed"), or is it one of delay, nit picking analysis, and resistance?

2. Does your ruling board try to solve every problem (are they micro-managers)? Or do they trust committees, staff, and others to initiate ministry and resolve the issues necessary to maintain and advance ministry endeavors?

3. List the ways in which you are permission givers (illustrate with specifics) or permission withholders (illustrate with specifics).

Supporting Scripture

"While they were worshiping the Lord and fasting, the Holy Spirit said, 'Set apart for me Barnabas and Saul for the work to which I have called them.' So after they had fasted and prayed, they placed their hands on them and sent them off." (Acts 13:2-3)

"The whole assembly became silent as they listened to Barnabas and Paul telling about the miraculous signs and wonders God had done among the Gentiles through them. When they finished, James spoke up: 'Brothers, listen to me. Simon has described to us how God at first showed his concern by taking from the Gentiles a people for himself. The words of the prophets are in agreement with this, as it is written:

"After this I will return and rebuild David's fallen tent. Its ruins I will rebuild, and I will restore it, that the remnant of men may seek the Lord, and all the

Gentiles who bear my name, says the Lord, who does these things" that have been known for ages.

'It is my judgment, therefore, that we should not make it difficult for the Gentiles who are turning to God. Instead we should write to them, telling them to abstain from food polluted by idols, from sexual immorality, from the meat of strangled animals and from blood.'" (Acts 15:12-20)

---

12. Shift from a pastor-centered/officer-centered ministry to shared ministry among pastor, officers, and congregation.

Today's church frequently accomplishes ministry through pastors and church officers (elders, deacons, and their equivalents). Pastors, officers, *and the whole people of God* share ministry in the transformational church. Pastors and officers become the permission-giving "equippers" and "senders" of every person to ministry.

The shift to transformational ministry is the shift from the leaders-do-it-all model to true delegation and permission-giving ministry. In other words, the shift is from a board-centered ministry (elders, deacons, vestry, council) to a member-centered ministry. In the traditional "officers do the ministry" church, it is not unusual to see fairly large boards. In a typical congregation with governing bodies of thirty elders and thirty deacons, I saw every major ministry committee — from Christian education to stewardship — draw half of its members from the elders and the other half from the deacons. Ministry was something church officers did. Everyone else watched. Furthermore, ministry was something they did almost entirely in the church building. Some "at-large" members of the congregation engaged in ministry, of course, but the emphasis was on church officers.

We have taught a generation of churchgoers that ministry is either "what the minister does" or leading as a church officer and participating in church programs (worship services, Sunday school, Vacation Bible School, youth groups, women's and men's ministries, service ministries). The implication is that members have a ministry if they are on the program leadership committee or the ministry team for some group or event, or if they participate in such groups or events. As far as involvement in the organized church goes, those are fine things, good things to do. But it means that only about 20 percent of the typical congregation "have a ministry" at any given time, and the other 80 percent are on the sidelines.

Furthermore, no matter how involved one may be in church activities, they occupy only a small percentage of one's total life. When we limit ministry to church programs, we fail to understand that ministry is first and foremost a way of life. Ministry is a lifestyle to be *lived out* wherever we are — in our homes, in the workplace, in our community — and therefore involves far more than the programs we lead and attend. Ministry is what we do to serve other people on behalf of Jesus Christ, wherever we may be, twenty-four hours a day.

Richard C. Halverson, former chaplain of the U.S. Senate, put it very clearly in a speech I heard him give at a men's prayer breakfast several years ago:

The maximum impact of the church of Jesus Christ in history in the world is not the impact of great and eloquent preachers, or denominations, or church hierarchies, or even popes, or priests, or cardinals, or all of the programs that the church invented. The maximum impact of the church of Jesus Christ is the influence of the aggregate of believers where they are between Sundays.

The measure of the effectiveness of a local church is not when the sanctuary is full on Sunday morning, and the programs are in operation. The measure of the effectiveness of the church is what's happening when the sanctuary is empty, the parking lot is empty, and the programs are not in operation, and people are scattered all over a metropolitan area, penetrating all of the organizations and institutions of that area, because where they are Christ is — in them. You are the church.

One of the most helpful developments advancing the ministry of every believer within the church today is the equipping church movement. Equipping ministry aims to develop and deploy every believer in the ministries that utilize the believer's willingness to serve, that fulfill the believer's passion and interests in ministry, and that engage the believer's gifts, talents, and experience.[3] To equip and send to ministry is, of course, the "Send" stage of the defining vision "Reach — Grow — Send." The model for this ministry comes from Christ himself: "It was he [Jesus] who gave some to be apostles, some to be prophets, some to be evangelists, and some to pastors and teachers, to prepare [equip] God's people for works of service, so that the body of Christ may be built up" (Eph. 4:11-12). "Equipping" churches take the needed steps to connect each person with a specific ministry or mission

3. For a more thorough discussion, see Sue Mallory, *The Equipping Church* (Grand Rapids: Zondervan, 2001).

effort. Transformational ministry equips people in the gathered state of the church for their lives and ministries both in the gathered state and in the scattered state — at home, in the workplace, and in the community. Plan your ministry to equip and provide your people with the knowledge and skills they need to grow in the character and lifestyle of Jesus Christ.

QUESTIONS FOR REFLECTION AND DISCUSSION

1. Are your decision-making committees, other than the ruling board, made up of church officers, or are they made up largely of members of the congregation? Remember, the more individuals and groups have the freedom to envision and initiate ministry, the more vital ministry will grow.

2. Do your elders or deacons set policy and do ministry by running programs, or do they set policy and send others to do ministry (participating themselves where they have particular interests and gifts)?

3. How can you take "the ministry of every believer" more seriously? Consider developing an equipping ministry to help people discover their passions and gifts for ministry and help them get engaged in actual ministry.

4. How can you help participants in the life of your congregation to "see themselves as sent" in all humility to ministry in the home, the workplace, and the community as well as within the program activities of the church?

Supporting Scripture

"It was he who gave some to be apostles, some to be prophets, some to be evangelists, and some to be pastors and teachers, to prepare God's people for works of service, so that the body of Christ may be built up until we all reach unity in the faith and in the knowledge of the Son of God and become mature, attaining to the whole measure of the fullness of Christ." (Ephesians 4:11-13)

"But you are a chosen people, a royal priesthood, a holy nation, a people belonging to God, that you may declare the praises of him who called you out of darkness into his wonderful light." (1 Peter 2:9)

CHAPTER SEVEN

Deciding on Your Next Steps

As a pastor or another leader in your congregation, you face a constant stream of demands coming from people with varying pastoral needs and from the requirements of the organization and program of your church. This seems to be what life is like for just about everyone involved in congregational ministry today. All of us have about as much to do as we can manage.

Since the development of a vital ministry and a transformational church will require changes in some present endeavors as well as the addition of new endeavors, certain considerations become essential. These considerations include your assessment of the present needs within your congregation, potential new ministries, goals and dreams you or others in your congregation may have, your level of responsibility for the church's ministry, your own schedule and energy level, the available resources (leadership, money, facilities), and current priorities.

Put simply, there is far more to do than can ever be done in ministry. The key is to discern those initiatives that will touch as many people as possible with discipleship-building and need-responding ministry within the limits of your resources. "Bless what is" (unless it is so dysfunctional that its continued operation will hurt the church) and "add what isn't."

Lewis Christiansen is a friend of mine who was a young man early in this century, when people still used a team of horses to pull a wagon. He remembers that as the weight of the wagon increased, more horses were added to the team. In a similar way, you may grow transformational ministry by "adding one horse at a time" — that is, by systematically adding one ministry endeavor or emphasis after another as you expand the scope of the ministry. To attempt to change everything at once is tempting, yet practically impossible.

Think in terms of both *sustaining vision* and *advancing vision*. *Sustaining vision* seeks to sustain with excellence those ministries that already exist in your congregation and that are helping build disciples and meet needs. Use the seven vital signs reviewed in shift number two to reshape and sustain your church's existing ministry programs. Use the twelve dynamic shifts as a guide to discerning *advancing vision* — the new ministry endeavors, emphases, and goals you will add to expand and enrich the ministry of your congregation.

Getting Started

In the game of football, one strategy for moving the ball down the field is to take what the defense gives you. If they prevent the pass, run with the ball. If they stop the long pass, make short ones. This strategy, which involves responsiveness and flexibility, is one you can use in your efforts to implement shifts in your church. In the beginning, make the changes and additions that look like they will bear the most fruit with the least resistance. This will permit you to celebrate some victories as you begin to undertake the more challenging shifts.

As you work to transform your church, don't get hung up by insisting that one or two of the twelve shifts offered here are the only ones or the very best ones for you to undertake now. Perhaps they are the most suitable places to start, but if you find it difficult to lead people to embrace those shifts, then choose others with which to move ahead. If your leaders and opinion-makers frown on "tinkering with the worship service," then bless what you have and start somewhere else. Work at adding new groups — entry-point groups and small groups in particular. Add the dimension of hospitality to the friendliness your church already shows. Or work at becoming "permission-giving." Eventually you can address all of the shifts.

To lead the church "as it is" requires one level of effort. To lead the church to change, to move to a new vitality, will require a greater level of effort. It may surprise you to know that only 10 percent of effective leadership has to do with discerning the vision, the goals, the plans. Most of your leadership efforts will have to do with the "how." How will you approach the congregation about change? Who will you need to get on board in a public meeting or in a one-to-one situation? What appropriate, nondefensive approach will you take with those who disagree? I encourage you to study this material, think through one or two next steps, and then read and study the material with your ruling board or decision-making committees. Propose the one or two next steps you believe are wise, and speak to people personally if necessary to get them on board. Assume that the board or other leaders may modify your proposal, perhaps adding or deleting a step, but that your leadership and forthright vision will help get all the members of your team moving in the same direction.

Deciding on Your Next Steps

Be prayerful. Ask God for vision and help. Depend on God for the next step. Have the high expectation that God has great plans for your congregation. And be patient. Recall how the former pastor of the congregation I serve gently chided me for being impatient when I was frustrated with the slowness of change: "That church didn't get where it was in a day." New life in the church will take the application of a transformational approach to ministry over a long period of time.

Remember, too, that a move toward change will be both exhilarating and frustrating. I received the following note from a woman who attended my seminar "Growing a Vital Church."® Her congregation is in the beginning throes of implementing a move to a new vitality. Both her sense of excitement and her sense of frustration are feelings you can expect to experience as you begin to seek change in your own fellowship:

> I'd like to update you on what's happened since Judy, Sue, and I attended the seminar in June. We came home with a vision of sharing three goals with the congregation: (1) apprentice leaders for all leadership positions, (2) Word-share-prayer in as many ministry team meetings as possible, and (3) the beginning of a small-group ministry. We have not been successful with the apprentice leader idea. We are still "using" leaders, frantic about trying to make people serve where we feel the church needs them (especially in the area of finance and nominations). This has been extremely frustrating to us. Although the leadership team says they agree with the concept, we are still not willing to slow down enough to spend time developing leaders. I am hoping to be able to model this with Maureen (our new small-group apprentice leader).

Personally, I am finding it difficult to be patient. I feel like I am not doing a good job of sharing the vision of what it can mean to have leaders who are passionate about their contributions.

As you can tell, I am seeing 20/20 how difficult this is. I believe with my whole heart that if churches are to become vital forces in the lives of individuals and communities, they must be willing to make the shifts suggested. . . . Each one makes so much sense. But each one is such a challenge. I feel the burden of interpretation and implementation. It is difficult not to become discouraged. I pray for the strength to continue. With the Holy Spirit at our side, we carry on!

What if others in your congregation don't share your vision or the vision in this book? Work at finding an alternate means of communicating the vision, such as by attending a seminar or vision-giving event together. Or maybe you can bring in someone who will affirm the history and dignity of your congregation's present life while pointing you together in a new direction. Try visiting one or more congregations that have vigorous transformational ministries, taking along with you people in whom you wish to inspire vision for a transformational congregation. Talk with the leaders you meet and glean the concept of ministry — the defining vision and defining practices — that are shaping the life of their congregations. Then look for specific ways to shape your own ministry with what you learn.

From the wonderful *Chronicles of Narnia* by C. S. Lewis, we glean this challenge: "Take the adventure the Lord has for you!" As you discern new vision, I urge you to take that adventure, trusting God for wisdom, blessing, and encouragement.

CHAPTER EIGHT

Implementing the Twelve Shifts: Some Examples

I follow with interest those who have attended my seminars on congregational vitality and leadership development, and I try to monitor the progress of congregations implementing the twelve shifts in their ministries. Examples of difficulties and successes that some of these churches have encountered may help you as you consider these shifts and attempt to work them into your own congregations.

Shift 1 (to embracing the high expectation that God has a vital future for your church)

Making that first shift to "high expectations" can be a difficult one, as the new pastor of a smaller congregation found out. He described an encounter with the elders over money, a common issue. He sat across the table from three retired men in dark suits who embraced their purpose as the men who "kept an eye on the money." Their concerns were real. At that time they were completing three years of deficit spending, and they feared that the congregation wouldn't be able to provide the resources for the coming year.

Their pastor began the arduous task of encouraging

them to raise their expectations, to believe that God had a vital future for their church. He finally convinced them, and together they developed and embarked upon a challenging campaign to raise capital. Through their enthusiastic commitment and energy, they were able to pass their vision on to the congregation, which joined them in raising $650,000 for a building addition and $65,000 for missions in less than six years. Through their efforts, the congregation changed from one whose elders were asking what should be cut from the budget to a congregation seeking ways to expand the ministry of Christ through their church.

Shift 2 (to implementing a vision for ministry),
Shift 3 (to embracing a sustaining and advancing vision),
Shift 6 (to an emphasis on communal and missional life),
and Shift 11 (to a permission-giving leadership)

Change is always hard, but it can be very rewarding, as the following examples show.

A good example of a difficult but ultimately rewarding encounter with change came from a congregation which assumed that "last year's programs would always be next year's ministry." The discipleship team reported to the elders that they had decided not to hold Vacation Bible School the following year because of some new and greater opportunities for ministry. They wished to put more effort and energy into a new midweek program for children of elementary-school age. The initial reaction of the elders was disapproval. "Who made this decision?" they asked. After some dialogue, however, they remembered that the discipleship team, which was responsible for Vacation Bible School, had been given the freedom to use the resources granted to their committee to carry out the overall mission of the church in the way they considered most effective. So in the end the elders supported the team's decision. This bolstered the team's confidence, and their new effort was a success, resulting in greater outreach for the church.

Another church decided to substitute for Vacation Bible School a week of study and fellowship for all ages in the church. This program was held in the evenings and included supper so that whole families could attend together. This was another success story.

Still another church changed the usual format of Vacation Bible School. They switched from meeting in church classrooms to meeting in a creative outdoor setting that depicted a city street in Jerusalem during Bible times, complete with shops and animals. Both children and adults dramatized the day-to-day activities. In fact, a range of adults from the congregation participated — parents, professionals, people on their lunch breaks, retired people. It proved to be an overwhelmingly positive experience for everyone.

The point here is not how each congregation changed their approach to Vacation Bible School. The point is the transformative power of the freedom to try new ministry approaches in churches with permission-giving leadership. These congregations were willing to shift from merely running old programs to implmenting new visions. Creative thinking, support, and participation from many parts of the congregation made these new ideas real and rewarding.

Shift 7 (to a ministry of worship and music responsive to the variety of needs present in the congregation and the community you are trying to reach) and Shift 9 (to adding new groups)

Another congregation experienced some difficulty making changes in the music program — always a touchy subject.

The chancel choir was losing members at the same time that a number of young people were straining for a chance to do something "new" in worship. In response to these needs, the congregation established a "worship team" of youth and young adults to lead worship once a month. This attracted the youth — who experimented with music, including guitar music — and gave the chancel choir a well-deserved week off. Around that time their organist left, and they were able to use the worship team and the guitar music for several weeks as a part of their substitute strategy. When the new director of music ministries came, he not only encouraged the continuation of the worship team but also invited the youth to be part of the chancel choir. The choir became stronger, the worship became more diverse, and more people became involved in the music ministry of the congregation. They're even publishing a contemporary worship resource. A member of that congregation said to the pastor, "I used to be able to skip church when I knew you weren't going to be there, but now I can't even do that. I'm afraid I might miss something!"

Shift 7 (to a ministry of worship and music responsive to the variety of needs present in the congregation and the community you are trying to reach)

For some churches, changes in worship and/or music carry the risk that some members will leave. One such church, which very gradually introduced different music into a Sunday-morning worship service, received support from most of the congregation but lost a few members. The pastor made follow-up calls on each of these members. One man made a very blunt and honest comment: "Unless you can tell me we're going back to the way things used to be, we have nothing to discuss." The pastor replied that he couldn't honestly say that. The man concluded, "I didn't think you could. Please know that I'm not saying that I'm right in this matter or that you're right. I'm just saying that I won't be there." The pastor thanked God for this man's integrity and his decision not to be divisive in the church. In this situation, choosing gradual change and paying attention to the feelings of all members of the congregation prevented more harmful problems. Today the worship services in this congregation are upbeat and well-attended.

Shift 8 (to a balance of audience-oriented ministry and face-to-face ministry) and Shift 2 (to implementing a vision for ministry)

Incorporating small groups and face-to-face ministry in a church enables true "community" and the deeper growth of personal relationships. One church ended their monthly "Lunch and Learn" meeting of retirees upon discovering that it had become strictly social and that planning and preparing meals and entertainment had become a burden to the leaders. After a year of "mourning," a committee asked the seniors what they really wanted and needed. In response they developed a program that's both simpler and more meaningful for the group. The seniors visit over bowls of homemade soup, then have a Bible study and share their concerns.

Shift 8 (to a balance of audience-oriented ministry and face-to-face ministry)

Small groups help develop the close relationships that are so important for members of a church. Several churches that I know of have begun seasonal small groups that meet during

Lent or Advent for study, reflection, and support. As the four to seven weeks of the seasonal small-group meetings draw to a close, each group member is asked if he or she would like to continue — and many say yes. Many ongoing small groups in the life of the church are generated this way, lasting not for a few weeks but for years. Extensive literature on launching small groups in congregations is proving useful and time-tested.

Shift 4 (to a ministry of friendliness and hospitality)

Emphasis on both hospitality and friendliness has been a challenge — but a rewarding one — for many churches. One congregation offered a free dinner to anyone who would come to the church on Thanksgiving Day. Several members of the church and several people from the community came. One man who had never attended the church said, "I can't wait to go home and call my daughter. I thought this would be a cafeteria-style meal around long tables, just eating and then going home. Instead this has been more like a family meal."

Shift 4 (to a ministry of friendliness and hospitality), Shift 7 (to a ministry of worship and music responsive to the variety of needs present in the congregation and the community you are trying to reach), Shift 5 (to developing discipleship), and Shift 12 (to shared ministry among pastor, officers, and congregation)

One congregation, realizing that many visitors were not familiar with their order of worship, changed the wording of the printed bulletin to be more helpful to unchurched guests. In addition, they have incorporated into the worship service an "Invitation to Christian Discipleship" to encourage people to make a conscious decision to follow Christ. Although they don't ask people to raise their hands or come to the front, they do make this a serious time for the entire congregation to consider their level of discipleship. They have also developed several "entry level" small groups, more Sunday school options for adults, and a one-on-one mentoring program for teens. This church has made a conscious effort to make every program an opportunity for people to learn about faith, and it has taught its members to share their own faith in God.

Shift 10 (to a "leader-developing" ministry, from committees to ministry teams), Shift 11 (to a permission-giving leadership), and Shift 12 (to shared ministry among pastor, officers, and congregation)

Many churches have reported that the most difficult shifts are those involving leadership, such as the shift from a "leader-using" ministry to a "leader-developing" ministry, the shift from a controlling to a permission-giving leadership, and the shift from a pastor-centered/officer-centered ministry to shared ministry among pastors, officers, and members. One church that has been successful in these areas moved from an eighteen-member board of elders that did all the work (and was difficult to fill) to a twelve-member group that enthusiastically leads church members into ministry within and beyond the congregation. By saying "yes" to ideas from members and empowering them to actively engage in ministry, the elders reduced their own workload and were freer to care for one another and the members of the congregation. Now members are blessed and "sent" by those elders to take meals to a women's shelter, organize blood drives, develop creative new programs, and care for each other in new, supportive ways.

Your congregation, like these churches and many others, will discover that through extensive planning and hard work, the twelve shifts may be employed to attract new members, increase active participation, grow the budget, and extend the outreach of your church. These congregations developed and began actively bringing forth exciting, vital visions for the future of their churches. I invite you and your congregation to also make the shift to the high expectation that God has a vital future for your church.

CONCLUSION

We have been looking at twelve shifts that can transform your congregation. Perhaps by now you are getting the idea behind all of them. First, bless the church as it is today. Have the grace to embrace the congregation's past and present ministries, including the people and the pastors who have served and are serving today. Show honor to their service, their philosophy, their programs and ministries, and embrace them by expressing appreciation. First, bless the congregation, and second, add new vision. Embrace those shifts in vision for ministry, in program and activity, that will permit the people already involved to be more deeply served and encouraged and that will reach those who are presently uninvolved or uncommitted to our Lord.

If the people you lead or the people who lead you simply have a vision for the vitality of the church that is different from yours, then seek ways you can fit in and make a significant supportive contribution to the vision that is there now. There are many ways to envision congregational vitality and several approaches to make it happen by God's grace and with God's help. However, a transformational church will not result from a critical or divisive spirit that comes from competing ideas about vitality. You say, "But I have a right to my vision!" Maybe so, but you don't have a mandate to cause division. The Spirit never acts in a manner that causes disunity. Look for "what the defense gives you" (to call on an earlier example) and press forward with the vision and ministry that will create a fresh vitality, depending completely on the Spirit of God for guidance and for the fruit to come. "Make every effort to keep the unity of the Spirit through the bond of peace" (Eph. 4:3).

Of course, I know you realize that the transformational church is already here in part. All of our congregations have elements of vitality. There are many congregations that have already moved deeply into the shifts required to make the transition from the present traditional church to the transformational church. Note that the transformational church does not set aside or do away with the major practices of the traditional church or devalue them in any way. The transformational church simply adds. It advances from leader-using to leader-using *and* leader-developing, from friendliness to friendliness *and* hospitality, from maintaining old groups to sustaining old groups *and* adding new groups, from audience-oriented groups to audience-oriented *and* face-to-face groups, and so on. *Bless and add.* Bless the past, and then add new ministry that will bring the future into today.

What is the best way to move your church from its present practice toward the practices of the transformational church? There are three questions to consider: (1) Are you willing to trust God for a transformational future for your church? (2) What is your vision for the transformational church, and what specific initial steps will you take in the coming year? and (3) Do you have the courage to change, and are you willing to pay the price of change?

One very effective way to bring the transformational church into the present is for a pastor and the elders and a variety of interested others to go as a team to some event in which the vision for a vigorous future church will be clearly presented. Many vital congregations and church consulting groups offer seminars on vital congregational dynamics. Take a team and go. (Don't go alone.)

Never forget that Jesus said, "I will build *my* church" (Matt. 16:18). The transition of your congregation into the transformational church depends on God's Spirit working through you and many others. Be urgent and earnest in prayer, seeking the Spirit's guidance. Jesus also said, "You do not have, because you do not ask God" (James 4:2b). Ask God to bring life and vitality, a vision for the future and hope for its realization into the life of your congregation.

A variety of ways reach people and help them grow in a meaningful relationship with Jesus Christ and into a vital congregation of Christ's people. However, some ways are simply more effective than others. We need to say, "Some of the old furniture in our congregations is no longer adequate for the task at hand. We do have wonderful memories, but it's time to move on." God bless you as you continue the process and the challenge of bringing vitality into the life of your congregation.

Make the Shift to the
Transformational Church in Your Church

Ask and trust God to work a new work among you.

Bless your ministry! Be grateful for all that God has done in, among, and through your congregation in the past. Rejoice in what God is doing right now.

Add to your ministry! Use the twelve shifts described here as a template or a set of lenses through which to look at your present ministry and see how it can be increased and enriched.

Adopt the shifts gradually. Don't attempt to address all of them at once. Choose two or at most three that you believe will be most helpful to your congregation's life at this time. Do some reflective planning with other leaders. Discern where you want to be in a year or two, develop a checklist of specific steps, and then get to work!

"Be strong and courageous, and do the work" (1 Chron. 28:20).

TWELVE DYNAMIC SHIFTS TO THE TRANSFORMATIONAL CHURCH

Shifts concerning Vision and Expectation

- First Shift — *from* your present aspiration for your congregation's future *to* the high expectation that God has a vital future for your church.
- Second Shift — *from* merely running programs *to* implementing a vision for ministry.
- Third Shift — *from* a maintenance mentality *to* a sustaining and advancing vision.

Shifts concerning Ministry to People

- Fourth Shift — *from* an emphasis on friendliness *to* a ministry of friendliness and hospitality.
- Fifth Shift — *from* assuming discipleship *to* developing discipleship.
- Sixth Shift — *from* a primary emphasis on the communal life of the church *to* a balanced emphasis on the communal and missional life of the church.

Shifts concerning Congregational Program

- Seventh Shift — *from* an unchanging worship format *to* a ministry of worship and music responsive to the variety of needs present in the congregation and the community you are trying to reach.
- Eighth Shift — *from* primarily audience-oriented programming (such as worship services, classes) *to* a balance of audience-oriented ministry and face-to-face ministry (such as small groups, one-on-one spiritual direction).
- Ninth Shift — *from* adding new people to established groups *to* adding new groups.

Shifts concerning the Practice of Leadership

- Tenth Shift — *from* a "leader-deploying" ministry *to* a "leader-developing" ministry, from committees to ministry teams.
- Eleventh Shift — *from* a controlling leadership *to* a permission-giving leadership.
- Twelfth Shift — *from* a pastor-centered/officer-centered ministry *to* shared ministry among pastor, officers, and congregation.

INFORMATION ON THE VITAL
CHURCHES INSTITUTE

E. Stanley Ott is pastor of the Pleasant Hills Community Presbyterian Church and president of the Vital Churches Institute and Vital Faith Resources.

The Vital Churches Institute serves to enable growth in the vitality and effectiveness of the local church. The institute offers seminars on principles and practices of personal spiritual growth and of vital congregational life, such as "Growing a Vital Church"® and "Developing Leadership for the Vital Church." The institute offers materials on these subjects through Vital Faith Resources. To learn more about The Vital Churches Institute and Vital Faith Resources, access the following Web sites:

http://www.vitalchurches.com
and
http://www.vitalfaithresources.com

You may correspond with Stan at *estanleyott@vitalchurches .com*. To receive Stan's weekly letter of encouragement, go to *www.buildingoneanother.com*.

For information on the seminars, or to order additional copies of this book and other materials to help you grow a vital church, you can send an e-mail to *info@vitalchurches.com,* or write to this address:

The Vital Churches Institute
P.O. Box 18378
Pittsburgh PA 15236
http://www.vitalchurches.com

RESOURCES FOR A
TRANSFORMATIONAL MINISTRY

First Shift: *from* your present hopes for your congregation's future *to* the high expectation that God has a vital future for your church

Galloway, Dale, ed. *Leading with Vision*. Kansas City: Beacon Hill Press, 1999.

Johnson, Ben Campbell, and Glenn McDonald. *Imagining a Church in the Spirit: A Task for Mainline Congregations*. Grand Rapids: Eerdmans, 1999.

Schuller, Robert H. *Move Ahead with Possibility Thinking*. New York: Jove Books, 1986.

Second Shift: *from* merely running programs *to* implementing a vision for ministry

Bandy, Thomas G. *Moving Off the Map: A Field Guide to Changing the Congregation*. Nashville: Abingdon Press, 1998.

Calian, Carnegie Samuel. *Survival or Revival: Ten Keys to Church Vitality*. Louisville: Westminster John Knox Press, 1998.

Callahan, Kennon L. *Twelve Keys to an Effective Church*. San Francisco: Jossey-Bass, 1983.

Chesnut, Robert A. *Transforming the Mainline Church*. Louisville: Geneva, 2000.

Coalter, Milton J.; John M. Mulder; and Louis B. Weeks. *Vital Signs: The Promise of Mainstream Protestantism.* Grand Rapids: Eerdmans, 1996.

Collins, James C., and Jerry I. Porras. *Built to Last: Successful Habits of Visionary Companies.* New York: HarperBusiness, 1997.

Easum, William, and Thomas G. Bandy. *Growing Spiritual Redwoods.* Nashville: Abingdon Press, 1997.

Edington, Howard, and Lyle E. Schaller. *Downtown Church: The Heart of the City.* Innovators in Ministry. Nashville: Abingdon Press, 1996.

Logan, Robert E. *Beyond Church Growth: Action Plans for Developing a Dynamic Church.* Tarrytown: Fleming H. Revell, 1989.

McIntosh, Gary L. *One Size Doesn't Fit All.* Grand Rapids: Fleming H. Revell, 1999.

McLaren, Brian D. *The Church on the Other Side: Doing Ministry in the Postmodern Matrix.* Grand Rapids: Zondervan, 1998.

McManus, Erwin. *An Unstoppable Force: Daring to Become the Church God Had in Mind.* Loveland: Group Publishing, Inc., 2001.

Mead, Loren B. *The Once and Future Church.* Bethesda: The Alban Institute, 1993.

Miller, Herb. *The Vital Congregation.* Nashville: Abingdon Press, 1990.

Ott, E. Stanley. *Vision for a Vital Church.* Pittsburgh: www.vitalfaithresources.com.

Payne, Claude E., and Hamilton Beazely. *Reclaiming the Great Commission: A Practical Model for Transforming Denominations and Congregations.* San Francisco: Jossey-Bass, 2000.

Riddell, Mark; Mark Pierson; and Cathy Kirkpatrick. *The Prodigal Project: Journey into the Emerging Church.* Great Britain: SPCK, 2000.

Schuller, Robert H. *Your Church Has Real Possibilities.* Ventura: Regal Books, 1974.

Schwarz, Christian A. *Natural Church Development: A Guide to Eight Essential Qualities of Healthy Churches.* St. Charles: ChurchSmart Resources, 1986.

Smith, Chuck, Jr. *The End of the World as We Know It: Clear Direction for Bold and Innovative Ministry in a Postmodern World.* Colorado Springs: Waterbrook Press, 2001.

Sweet, Leonard. *Aquachurch: Essential Leadership Arts for Piloting Your Church in Today's Fluid Culture.* Loveland: Group Publishing, Inc., 1999.

———. *Carpe Mañana: Is Your Church Ready to Seize Tomorrow?* Grand Rapids: Zondervan, 2001.

Warren, Rick. *The Purpose-Driven Church.* Grand Rapids: Zondervan, 1995.

Third Shift: *from* a maintenance mentality *to* a sustaining and advancing vision

Barna, George. *The Power of Vision: How You Can Capture and Apply God's Vision for Your Ministry.* Ventura: Regal Books, 1997.

———. *Turn-Around Churches: How to Overcome Barriers to Growth and Bring New Life to an Established Church.* Ventura: Regal Books, 1997.

———. *Turning Vision into Action.* Ventura: Regal Books, 1997.

Biehl, Bob. *Masterplanning: A Complete Guide for Building a Strategic Plan for Your Business, Church, or Organization.* Nashville: Broadman & Holman, 1997.

Gibbs, Eddie. *ChurchNext: Quantum Changes in How We Do Ministry.* Downers Grove: InterVarsity Press, 2000.

Leadership Training Network. *Assessing Church Culture.* www.LTN.org.

Malphurs, Aubrey. *Advanced Strategic Planning: A New Model for Church and Ministry Leaders.* Grand Rapids: Baker Book House, 1999.

Nanus, Burt. *Visionary Leadership: Creating a Compelling Sense of Direction for Your Organization.* San Francisco: Jossey-Bass, 1995.

Odiorne, George S. *Management and the Activity Trap.* New York: Harper & Row, 1974.

Shelley, Marshal. *Renewing Your Church through Vision and Planning: Thirty Strategies to Transform Your Ministry.* The Library of Leadership Development, vol. 2. Minneapolis: Bethany House, 1997.

Southerland, Dan. *Transitioning: Leading Your Church Through Change*. Grand Rapids: Zondervan, 2000.

Fourth Shift: *from* an emphasis on friendliness *to* a ministry of friendliness and hospitality

Barna, George. *User-Friendly Churches: What Christians Need to Know about the Churches People Love to Go to*. Ventura: Regal Books, 1991.

Bernhard, Fred. *Widening the Welcome of Your Church: Biblical Hospitality and the Vital Congregaton*. Fort Wayne: Christian Community, 1996.

Geitz, Elizabeth Rankin. *Entertaining Angels: Hospitality Programs for the Caring Church*. Harrisburg: Morehouse Publishing, 1993.

Greig, Doris W. *We Didn't Know They Were Angels: Discovering the Gift of Christian Hospitality*. Ventura: Regal Books, 1987.

Schaller, Lyle E., and Edward Lee Tucker. *Forty-Four Ways to Increase Church Attendance*. Nashville: Abingdon Press, 1988.

Fifth Shift: *from* assuming discipleship *to* developing discipleship

Barna, George. *Growing True Disciples: New Strategies for Producing Genuine Followers of Christ*. Colorado Springs: Waterbrook Press, 2001.

Foster, Richard. *Celebration of Discipline: The Path to Spiritual Growth*. New York: Harper & Row, 1978.

Hybels, Bill, and Mark Mittelberg. *Becoming a Contagious Christian*. Grand Rapids: Zondervan, 1996.

Linn, Jan G. *Re-Claiming Evangelism: A Practical Guide for Mainline Churches*. St. Louis: Chalice, 1998.

McLaren, Brian D. *A New Kind of Christian*. San Francisco: Jossey-Bass, 2001.

Ogden, Greg. *Discipleship Essentials*. Downers Grove: InterVarsity Press, 1998.

Ott, E. Stanley. *The Joy of Discipling*. Grand Rapids: Zondervan, 1989 (available from www.vitalfaithresources.com).

Willard, Dallas. *The Divine Conspiracy: Rediscovering Our Hidden Life in God.* New York: HarperCollins, 1999.

————. *The Spirit of the Disciplines: Understanding How God Changes Lives.* San Francisco: Harper & Row, 1988.

Sixth Shift: *from* a primary emphasis on the communal life of the church *to* a balanced emphasis on the communal and missional life of the church

Bosch, David J. *Transforming Mission: Paradigm Shifts in Theology of Mission.* Maryknoll: Orbis, 1991.

Guder, Darrell L. *The Continuing Conversion of the Church.* Grand Rapids: Eerdmans, 2000.

————, ed. *Missional Church: A Vision for the Sending of the Church in North America.* Grand Rapids: Eerdmans, 1998.

Hauerwas, Stanley, and William H. Willimon. *Resident Aliens: Life in the Christian Colony.* Nashville: Abingdon Press, 1989.

Pine, B. Joseph, and James H. Gilmore. *The Experience Economy: Work Is Theatre, and Every Business a Stage.* Boston: Harvard Business School Press, 1999.

Roxburgh, Alan. *The Missionary Congregation: Leadership and Liminality.* Harrisburg: Trinity Press International, 1997.

Sweet, Leonard. *Post-Modern Pilgrims.* Nashville: Broadman & Holman, 2000.

Seventh Shift: *from* an unchanging worship format *to* a ministry of worship and music responsive to the variety of needs present in the congregation and the community you are trying to reach

Callahan, Kennon L. *Dynamic Worship.* San Francisco: Jossey-Bass, 1997.

Miller, David A. *Contemporary Worship in the Reformed Tradition.* Pittsburgh: Vital Faith Resources, 2001.

Slaughter, Michael. *Out on the Edge: A Wake-Up Call for Church Leaders on the Edge of the Media Reformation.* Nashville: Abingdon Press, 1998.

Webber, Robert E. *Renew Your Worship: A Study in the Blending of Traditional and Contemporary Worship.* Peabody: Hendrickson Publishers, 1997.

Eighth Shift: *from* primarily audience-oriented programming *to* a balance of audience-oriented ministry and face-to-face ministry

Arnold, Jeffrey. *The Big Book on Small Groups.* Downers Grove: InterVarsity Press, 1992.

Donahue, Bill. *Leading Life-Changing Small Groups.* Grand Rapids: Zondervan, 1996.

George, Carl F. *Prepare Your Church for the Future.* Grand Rapids: Fleming H. Revell, 1995.

―――, with Warren Bird. *Nine Keys to Effective Small Group Leadership.* Mansfield: Kingdom Publishing, 1997.

Icenogle, Gareth. *Biblical Foundations for Small Group Ministry.* Downers Grove: InterVarsity Press, 1994.

Meyer, Richard C. *One Anothering,* vol. 1: *Biblical Building Blocks for Small Groups.* Philadelphia: Innisfree Press, 1990.

―――. *One Anothering,* vol. 2: *Building Spiritual Community in Small Groups.* Philadelphia: Innisfree Press, 1999.

―――. *One Anothering,* vol. 3: *Building Spiritual Community in Small Groups.* Philadelphia: Innisfree Press, 2002.

Ott, E. Stanley. *Small Group Life.* Pittsburgh: www.vitalfaithresources.com, 1994.

Ninth Shift: *from* adding new people to established groups *to* adding new groups

See the small-group resources above, as well as the following:

George, Carl F. *The Coming Church Revolution: Empowering Leaders for the Future.* Grand Rapids: Fleming H. Revell, 1994.

Kleissler, Thomas A.; Margo A. Lebert; and Mary C. McGuinness. *Small Christian Communities: A Vision of Hope for the Twenty-First Century.* Mahwah: Paulist Press, 1997.

Tenth Shift: *from* a "leader-deploying" ministry *to* a "leader-developing" ministry, from committees to ministry teams

Barna, George. *The Power of Team Leadership.* Colorado Springs: Waterbrook Press, 2001.

Blancard, Ken; Donald Carew; and Eunice Parisi. *The One-Minute Manager Builds High-Performance Teams.* New York: William Morrow, 2000.

Cladis, George. *The Team-Based Church.* San Francisco: Jossey-Bass, 1999.

Cordeiro, Wayne. *Doing Church as a Team.* Ventura: Regal Books, 2001.

Hestenes, Roberta. *Turning Committees into Communities.* Colorado Springs: Navpress, 1991.

Reeves, R. Daniel. "Practical Advice for Launching Teams." *Ministry Advantage,* vol. 8, no. 1 (Winter 1998). http://www.fuller.edu/cll/ma/ma8.1/html/reeves4.html.

Eleventh Shift: *from* a controlling leadership *to* a permission-giving leadership

Bandy, Thomas G. *Christian Chaos: Revolutionizing the Congregation.* Nashville: Abingdon Press, 1999.

Blanchard, Kenneth H., and Michael O'Connor. *Managing by Values.* San Francisco: Berrett-Koehler Publishers, 1997.

Collins, James C. *Good to Great: Why Some Companies Make the Leap . . . and Others Don't.* New York: HarperCollins, 2001.

Easum, William. *Leadership on the Other Side.* Nashville: Abingdon Press, 2000.

———. *Sacred Cows Make Gourmet Burgers: Ministry Anytime, Anywhere, by Anyone.* Nashville: Abingdon Press, 1995.

Kouzes, James, and Barry Posner. *Encouraging the Heart: A Leader's Guide to Rewarding and Recognizing Others.* San Francisco: Jossey-Bass, 1999.

Malphurs, Aubrey. *Values-Driven Leadership.* Grand Rapids: Baker Book House, 1996.

Twelfth Shift: *from* a pastor-centered/officer-centered ministry *to* shared ministry among pastor, officers, and congregation

Bugbee, Bruce; Don Cousin; and Bill Hybels. *Network: Understanding God's Design for You in the Church.* Grand Rapids: Zondervan, 1996.

Mallory, Sue. *The Equipping Church.* Grand Rapids: Zondervan, 2001.

———, and Brad Smith. *The Equipping Church Guidebook.* Grand Rapids: Zondervan, 2001. See also www.ltn.org.

Ogden, Greg. *The New Reformation: Returning the Ministry to the People of God.* Grand Rapids: Zondervan, 1992.

Change and Transition

Anderson, Leith. *Dying for Change.* Minneapolis: Bethany House, 1990.

Bandy, Thomas G. *Coaching Change.* Nashville: Abingdon Press, 2000.

Bridges, William. *Managing Transitions.* Cambridge: Perseus Books, 1991.

Herrington, Jim; Mike Bonem; and James H. Furr. *Leading Congregational Change.* San Francisco: Jossey-Bass, 2000.

Johnson, Spencer, M.D. *Who Moved My Cheese? An Amazing Way to Deal with Change in Your Work and in Your Life.* New York: Putnam, 1998.

Kotter, John P. *Leading Change.* Boston: Harvard Business School Press, 1996.

Mundey, Paul. *Unlocking Church Doors: Ten Keys to Positive Change.* Nashville: Abingdon Press, 1997.

Web sites

ALPHA North America: alphana@aol.com; international Web site: www.alpha.org.uk
Bill Easum and Tom Bandy: www.easumbandy.com
ChurchSmart: www.churchsmart.com
Leadership Network: www.ln.org

Leadership Training Network: www.ltn.org
Small Group Network: www.smallgroups.com
SpiritVenture: www.LeonardSweet.com
The Vital Churches Institute: www.vitalchurches.com/info
    @vitalchurches.com